PENGUIN BOOKS

DENALI

Ben Moon is an adventure and lifestyle photographer turned director and filmmaker who uses his intuitive sensibilities to bring individuals and their stories to life: from climbing and surfing images, to music videos, to behind-the-scenes narratives. For more than seventeen years his work has been featured in the pages of Patagonia catalogs, where he seeks to capture the beauty and authenticity of people challenging themselves everywhere, from the sheer rock walls of Yosemite to fifty-foot waves in the Pacific Northwest.

Because Ben is also a rock climber, surfer, and adventurer, his insights into the subjects he photographs are tangible. He takes this ability to connect with others a step further in his ongoing black-and-white portrait project called *Faces*, in which each individual's inner beauty is revealed in a disarming and intimate manner.

Founded in 2014, his production company, Moonhouse, is a platform for collaborating with like-minded friends and creatives who share his commitment to bringing thoughtful stories to life on-screen. The 2015 short film *Denali* told Ben's own deeply personal story about his battle with colorectal cancer and his relationship with his beloved dog Denali, who passed away from cancer a decade after Ben recovered from the disease. The film continues to touch new audiences online and at film festivals worldwide. Ben's most recent short films include *Offseason*, which features his close friend Daniel Norris, a pitcher for the Detroit Tigers, who lived in his van during past off-seasons, and *Grizzly Country*, which features ecowarrior and grizzly bear activist Doug Peacock.

Ben now lives in Pacific City, Oregon, where he explores the nearby dunes of Cape Kiwanda and shores of the Pacific Ocean with his pup, Nori, who has strikingly similar facial markings to Denali and shares many of his finer personality traits.

Denali

A Man, a Dog, and the

Friendship of a Lifetime

BEN MOON

PENGUIN BOOKS

PENGUIN BOOKS
An imprint of Penguin Random House LLC
penguinrandomhouse.com

LIBRARY OF CONGRESS CATALOGING-IN-PUBLICATION DATA

Names: Moon, Ben, author.
Title: Denali : a man, a dog, and the friendship of a lifetime / Ben Moon.
Description: New York : Penguin Books, [2020]
Identifiers: LCCN 2019033838 (print) | LCCN 2019033839 (ebook) |
ISBN 9780143133612 (paperback) | ISBN 9780525505419 (ebook)
Subjects: LCSH: Moon, Ben. | Dog owners—United States—Biography. |
Colon (Anatomy)—Cancer—Patients—United States—Biography. |
Dogs—United States—Biography. | Human-animal relationships.
Classification: LCC SF422.82.M66 A3 2020 (print) | LCC SF422.82.M66
(ebook) | DDC 636.70092/9—dc23
LC record available at https://lccn.loc.gov/2019033838
LC ebook record available at https://lccn.loc.gov/2019033839

Printed in the United States of America
1 3 5 7 9 10 8 6 4 2

Book design and title page photography by Daniel Lagin

A Second Opinion

And when someone you love walks in through the door,
even if it happens five times a day, go totally insane
with joy.

—DAVID DUDLEY

I f you decide against this procedure, Ben, the recurrence rate for your
tumor will be 50 percent or greater."

Dr. Ahmad's words echoed uncomfortably in my mind as I pointed
my van westward through Portland's rush-hour traffic toward the
coast. I'd come to him for a second opinion but received precisely the
worst-case news I'd feared. And now, I needed to get to the ocean—up
and over the coast range and away from the summer heat and the claus-
trophobia I always feel in cities—to wash off the surreal grime of it
all. Only a body of water as immense as the Pacific Ocean would be
powerful enough for the job.

Riding beside me was my beloved Denali, a handsome husky and pit bull mix who had been my constant companion for the past four and a half years. He had entered my life as an eight-week-old pup, finding me at a time when I felt ill-equipped to raise a puppy, yet fate saw that I needed his support and companionship more than anything. I had no idea how much I would lean on him through the trials that followed.

Almost exactly a year after bringing him home, my wife, Melanie, left me for another man and shattered my notions of the future. I was twenty-five years old and had little idea of what I was supposed to do with my life. Denali became the only friend with whom I could fully express my grief. He put up with my many tears and countless hugs, and as I struggled to make sense of this new reality, we became as inseparable as two souls can be.

When it became obvious that Melanie wasn't coming back, I packed up my belongings and, with Denali riding shotgun, set off to begin a job working for a climbing gear manufacturer located in the high-desert recreational town of Bend, Oregon. I sewed a bed for the back of my Subaru wagon utilizing fabric and foam for manufacturing bouldering crash pads (fold-up pads that can be carried to shorter climbs that do not require ropes and placed at the base to cushion falls), and Denali and I lived in the vehicle full time for nearly a year as I began a new career as an outdoor adventure photographer. Denali was the perfect roommate, burrowing underneath the covers when ice formed inside the windows. He would tuck in beside me, sharing warmth and love that slowly began to heal my crushed heart. Denali was never upset as I mused endlessly over the mysteries of women and heartache. Science now tells us that connecting with a dog lowers our cortisol while releasing oxytocin. Denali's nurturing devotion and its effects on me were a powerful testament to that.

I had been diagnosed with stage III colorectal cancer, a disease seldom associated with a twenty-nine-year-old. My visit to the gastrointestinal surgeon was for a second opinion about which procedure was appropriate to remove the cancerous mass. He was certain that removing my rectum and anus was necessary to ensure the proper healthy tissue margins and reduce the tumor's chances of recurring. Which meant, he said, that I would need a permanent colostomy. The idea of shitting into a plastic bag for the rest of my life was hard to fathom, especially considering my lifestyle revolved around rock climbing, surfing, and photographing high-level athletes in their element. I tensely awaited his recommendation, barely able to breathe as I prayed that he would tell me the colostomy was unnecessary.

The gravity of coming face-to-face with my mortality had knocked me way off center, and I suddenly found myself far from the rhythms of traveling between the climbing crags and surf breaks of the American west, photographing a tribe of like-minded people who valued a life of adventure over the creature comforts of a steady salary and a mortgage. In many ways, living on the road was easy, due to its lack of complexity. But the creative path has its own set of challenges, and I struggled mightily to make ends meet when first committing to go all-in on photography as my sole income. Even though a novice's freelance income was barely enough to fill the food bin in my van, the benefits of waking up far from the din of civilization in a place of my choosing and allowing the cycles of the sun and weather to dictate the activities of each day had its rewards. Chasing the magic hours of light and finding the perfect frame often brought me to places of breathtaking beauty and introduced lifelong friendships. This, and my life with Denali, became everything to me until cancer leaped out of the dark and grabbed me by the throat.

Colorectal cancer.

The word *cancer* alone was terrifying enough. I was unaware that the barrage of physical, emotional, and bureaucratic indignities endemic to the medical and insurance industries here in America would nearly drown me. In the prime of my twenties, I felt invincible. No one at that age anticipates a cancer diagnosis, much less a form of the disease usually associated with people far into their retirement years. Even more devastating to my young ego, colon cancer in particular carries both a stigma and symptoms that most people prefer not to discuss in public.

————

AS THE TRAFFIC GREW SPARSE AND SUBURBIA GAVE WAY TO COASTAL FORests, my mood lifted, and I began to anticipate a glimpse of the Pacific sparkling through the trees. During my childhood in western Michigan, Lake Michigan was my ocean. Near the south end of the lakeshore town of Grand Haven, there is a corner where the road crests above the dunes and where the view always hit me like a four-shot espresso as the expanse of the lake offered new breath to overcome whatever challenges I faced.

With the reality of the battle ahead beginning to sink in, reaching the Pacific was a welcome reminder that in spite of all that stood in front of me, there were much greater powers at play. My worries—an early death from cancer versus a long life burdened with wearing a shit bag—were somehow insignificant once I began to feel the pull of the currents and the tidal rhythms dictated by a moon that circled hundreds of thousands of miles above. We pulled up to a stretch of beach just north of the postcard-famous Haystack Rock at Cannon Beach, and as I stripped down to board shorts, Denali looked on with concern. He had always been tuned into my worries, often well before I was even aware of them, and he hadn't taken his eyes off me since I'd been diagnosed just days earlier. As I began to sprint across the sand and into the sea, every step jostled the shock deeper. My body, I knew, would never be the same with a poop bag hanging from my abdomen. Denali matched me stride for stride.

My pace slowed as the currents tugged at my waist, and I dove into the icy fifty-degree water. Coming up refreshed, I realized Denali was still beside me, swimming determinedly since, by now, it was much too deep for him to stand. Skin tingling from the cold baptism, I stood still, staring at the glowing horizon, my despair slowly shifting to a sense of determination.

A set of swollen waves appeared before us, and I saw Denali's eyes widen with the realization that he was outside his comfort zone. As the first wave neared, he spun and began swimming frantically toward the shore. He was driven by fear and yet in perfect sync with the wave, and as it caught him, he somehow slid down its face with the grace of a porpoise, the glassy surface continuing onward, pushing him along before releasing him in the shallows. I laughed out loud at the joy of seeing my pup catch his first wave and realized that there was a lesson in this: we're powerless to fight the unexpected swells in life, and there are times when the only choice is to let go of the perception that we're in control and simply allow the wave to carry us through.

I played the scenarios over and over in my mind. Would I be able to climb with a colostomy? Surf the waves I had yet to explore? Love a woman? Or have a woman be attracted to me? I hugged Denali, and he looked up at me with a confidence that gave me hope I would somehow make it through all this.

We'll ride out this wave, together, I thought. *Thank you, Denali.*

Denali

1

First Sight

A dog is foremost an instrument of personal growth: It exists to ease your existential anxieties, impart lessons about love and friendship, and teach you how to be a better person.

—DAVID DUDLEY

After completing a sports medicine program at Grand Valley State University, I moved from the Great Lakes to Oregon with Melanie, the woman I had just married at the wise, young age of twenty-three. She was twenty. Neither of us had ever visited the West Coast before, but the allure of the mountains and remote coastline of the Pacific Northwest seemed an apt reason to break free from the upper Midwest.

After the wedding ceremony, we settled in Grand Haven, long my favorite beach town, and it was there on Lake Michigan that I surfed my first waves, in the saltless, inland sea. In spite of that, I soon became restless living so close to where I had grown up, and craved those climbing crags that I saw in magazines. Poring over guides to the Pacific Northwest, I marveled at the impressive mountain peaks, plentiful climbing areas, and diverse recreational activities. I dreamed of moving west toward those mountains, the Pacific Ocean, and the adventures that I had only read about in guidebooks.

A few months after the wedding, an old friend moved to Aloha, Oregon. Wedged between Beaverton and Hillsboro and lined with chain stores and car dealerships, Aloha was an ill-fitting name for the industrial Portland suburb. During a phone call, I shared my desire to move west, and he offered to rent out a room in the apartment where he was staying. This seemed the perfect opportunity to make the move west I had been imagining.

Melanie and I packed up our possessions and crammed them all into our old Isuzu Rodeo, heading south on US 31. We navigated Chicago's urban sprawl and drove northwest until the long, westward straightaways of Interstate 94 drew us through the frozen plains of North Dakota before we stopped in Bozeman, Montana, for a night.

I felt a sense of relief as the west seemed to welcome us with its kind residents and stunning vistas. I stared in awe at the landscape of Coeur d'Alene, Idaho, before the power steering froze and the lights dimmed in the depressed village of Ritzville, Washington, as the alternator seized. It was the weekend, so we called every parts store until we found a mechanic who would bring a replacement down and install it the next morning.

As we ate at a divey but homey diner, our server asked where we were headed. "Portland!" I said, excited to be free of the flat and stifling Midwest. "Man, I wish I could leave this town," he said, dropping his head, "but I can't." I was baffled by that sense of resignation as memories played of my classmates finding factory jobs and moving in next door to their parents.

It was nightfall before Melanie and I drove our sputtering SUV over the Willamette River, crossing the Marquam Bridge in northwest Portland. A damp fog hung low and oppressive, obscuring most of the city. The record for the longest stretch of days without sunshine was broken over the three weeks that followed. "Welcome to Oregon," the road sign had read. In spite of the drear, I was psyched to be in a place that offered so much outdoor potential.

For our first three weeks in our new home in Aloha, a southwest suburb of Portland, the sun had yet to show itself. *Who named this place Aloha if there is no sunshine?!* I often thought. Our apartment was just off Canyon Road, and one morning, as I pulled out onto Canyon Road heading east toward downtown Portland, the sunshine finally pierced the gloom to reveal the stunning snow-covered outline of Mount Hood standing like a monument ahead. Despite nearly a month of living in Oregon, I had no idea there was a mountain so near. My heart soared at the thought of snowboarding those dazzling white slopes and climbing to its summit someday.

The following week, I stopped at a gear shop and noticed a Smith Rock climbing guidebook on the counter. After flipping through it, I asked the shop owner about it. "Looks like an amazing place to climb, is that near here? When's the best time to climb there?"

"Smith is about three hours southeast of here. It's an incredible area. You can climb there year-round as long as it's not snowing," he answered. My curiosity was piqued, and I bought the book on the spot. I did not know how much that special climbing area would mean to me in the years to come.

After I showed the book to Melanie, we agreed that a visit was in order, and drove the three hours over the Cascade Range, arriving at Smith Rock late one evening. It was completely black from the dense cloud cover. As we pitched the tent, I could feel a vast presence nearby, but had no visuals to fill in for my imagination. I slept restlessly, too excited by the prospect of a day exploring a true climbing area, a novelty in the Great Lakes where I had grown up. The high-desert air was filled with the unfamiliar smell of sage and another that was disconcertingly familiar. The air reeked with an odor that I later learned was juniper berries, but at the time only reminded me of the times when my mom's rescue kitty emptied his bladder on my bed and in the deepest corners of my closet.

At dawn, I unzipped the tent to relieve myself, and the view out the door was so shocking that I no longer felt the urge to piss. Instead, I tried to absorb the magnificence of the craggy amphitheater of reddish rock that surrounded the campsite. I stared down at the river that curved through the canyon, and in the early morning light, my eyes strained to find the climbable lines on the sheer faces. I was both euphoric and slightly nauseated with intimidation. These volcanic walls of welded tuff were so much more majestic than anything I'd ever seen or considered climbing.

"Traditional" crack climbing utilizes camming devices, or "cams," placed in parallel sided cracks, and "nuts," or small aluminum chocks, that are wedged into constrictions within the cracks. All of this gear is removed after the climb, whereas "sport climbing" depends on anchors permanently bolted to a rock wall, clipping ropes into quickdraws—two carabiners with a sling in between—that are clipped to the bolts on the rock face, spaced anywhere from three to twenty feet apart depending on the terrain. If you are five feet above your last clipped-in bolt, you'll fall a minimum of ten feet, plus the extra amount your weight stretches the rope before your fall is halted. Sport climbing tends to be on face climbs, where the hand- and footholds are small edges or pockets and where no cracks are safe enough to use removable cams or nuts.

To get a feel for the style of climbing on the sheer vertical cliffs, I tried a few easier routes to warm up and realized that the difficulty of the climbs at each grade was stout, and the spacing between the bolts to which I clipped my quickdraw were farther apart than I had ever experienced. Each time I found a stance to clip the next bolt, I realized that my feet were well over a full body length or more past my last point of protection, meaning that I would drop up to twenty feet if I fell. I gripped the small crimps tighter and tiptoed upward, hoping the sticky rubber on my climbing shoes would stay adhered to the tiny nubbins of rock that seemed likely to break at any moment from my body weight. I was so focused on getting to the anchors at the top of the climb that I missed one of the bolts. I was shaking from fear at the long loop of rope that seemed to hang loosely between the knot on my harness and the last point of protection far below. I took a deep breath and with numb fingers clipped into the anchors, breathed a sigh of relief. *Wow*, I thought, *this is what I moved out west for.*

As Melanie and I settled into our new marriage and new home in Oregon, I found myself yearning for a dog. I spent hours poring over dog books, researching breeds that would be best suited to the outdoor life I craved. A few breeds were more appealing than others, but I thought it would be unfair to adopt any dog until I fully realized my dream of spending my days rock climbing and exploring the beaches and deserts of the west.

The city's no place for a dog. I thought. *I need to wait until we move somewhere my dog and I can feel free. No traffic, no leash laws . . . just clean air, space to roam, and a life that allows us to be together all day.*

One Sunday in November, Melanie convinced me to stop by the local animal shelter with her, assuring me that it would be a flyby, just to see what kinds of dogs might be available when I was ready to adopt. Against my better instincts, I agreed, and soon we were walking the barren concrete halls of the Bonnie L. Hays Animal Shelter, overwhelmed by the cacophony of whining and crying dogs. A pile of sightless puppies crawled over one another to my right, and the sad, listless eyes of an abandoned senior stared opposite. I soon felt overcome by hopelessness and the pungent odor of antiseptic cleaners. All I could think about was getting out of that forlorn place. Looking for the exit, I rushed down a cage-lined aisle, already emotionally far away.

Suddenly, a puppy's calm stare stopped me in my tracks. He was sitting alone in a pen at eye level, watching me in silence. His inquisitive and calm presence caused my heart to spark and sputter to life. Surprised by the feeling in my chest, I stepped forward and continued past him. As I walked by, I heard a resolute "yip!" emerge from his cage. I knew he was speaking to me directly and was not going to let me pass without acknowledging the moment of connection we already had shared.

I sighed and whispered, "Okay, buddy, talk to me," as I stole a glance back at the pup. He was brown and black with symmetrical markings on his forehead, and had eyes that appeared rimmed with eyeliner. Lifting a paw, he offered it to me through the bars of his cage, drawing me nearer to him. Now that he had my full attention, he cocked his head, soft ears flopping to one side as he locked his big brown eyes with mine. His gaze was steady, already hinting at the personality of the old soul I would soon come to know.

Hey there. You look nice. Um, why can't you look at me? I just got dumped in this place! I need someone to set me free. It stinks in here and I'm sick of all the whining and barking. Sheesh.

Oh good, you're finally noticing me! Hi again. Whoa, you look like you could use a friend. Let me out of here and I'll love you forever.

Catching my breath, I glanced down at the name tag on his pen. It read:

BROOKLYN

LAB/PIT BULL MIX

MALE—8 WEEKS

Oh good, I thought. *This one might not be right for me.* I was momentarily relieved, as I had planned to adopt a female puppy, and a pit bull terrier was not a breed I had even considered. But as I stood there, I felt the stirrings of an undeniable bond already forming. I found a shelter attendant, who quickly summarized what he knew about Brooklyn's background. "There's been a lot of interest in this little guy. I doubt he'll be in here much longer," he said. "A lady adopted him from a neighbor's litter at six weeks, then brought him here two weeks later after they realized they couldn't handle a puppy."

"What about the pit bull part of him? And aren't male dogs more aggressive?" I asked lamely, searching for excuses to pass on him.

"Pit mixes can be amazing pets," the attendant said, "and if they're neutered and properly trained, males shouldn't have issues with aggression. His mother was a pit bull, but we don't know about the dad—a Labrador retriever is our best guess, but honestly, we have no idea. Want to take him out to the play area and see if you get along?"

I agreed, and we brought the pup to the other room to meet Melanie. After we closed the door, I removed the leash, and little Brooklyn ran around the perimeter of the concrete room, tearing past Melanie and the attendant before settling at my feet. He rolled onto his back, his legs splayed wide, and stared up at me with a confidence that hinted at the loyal friend he would become. As he chewed on my shoelace, I knew in my very soul that he and I were meant to be together—there was no doubt about it. All my previous hesitations melted away, and I knew in my heart that this furry being was going to be in my life for years to come.

THE FORMATIVE YEARS OF MY CHILDHOOD WERE SPENT OFF THE GRID, LIVING off the land deep within the forests of Michigan. Our family dogs became both my go-to adventure buddies and trusted confidants, and those years spent in the quiet of the forest with a dog at my side instilled in me a love for solitude and time outside in nature.

Growing up, I never went to a traditional church with a preacher. Instead, my family met in various homes each Sunday morning and Wednesday night, studying the teachings of Christ that served as the foundation of our faith. Before they adopted these beliefs, my parents had been a part of something far different.

My mom and dad first met in Colorado in their early twenties, at a meeting for a communal sect called the Children of God. They were married three weeks later. Once they joined, they were required to turn all their earthly possessions over to the cult leader. With only the clothes on their backs, my parents handed out pamphlets and asked for money on the streets as they roamed throughout the southern states of Alabama, Arizona, Texas, and Louisiana.

After a year, they became skeptical of the group's doctrines, and they broke free of the cult's brainwashing and moved back to my dad's home state of Michigan. They floated for a bit, eventually buying twenty forested acres in the rural western portion of the state using a loan from my grandparents. I was still an infant when they left the cult, so I have few memories until we settled on the property there, but my birth certificate still holds a mark from that time. Just above my current middle name of Robert, my given middle name from the sect is scratched out: Seeds. My parents had sworn off organized religion until a chance meeting with a couple of traveling ministers from a nondenominational faith helped them regain their spirituality.

Melanie's family was part of the same faith, and they quickly accepted me as one of their own soon after we met.

———

DURING MY CHILDHOOD, I WAS SENSITIVE. AS IN OVER-THE-TOP SENSITIVE. And as a highly sensitive kid, I absorbed my mother's anxiety. This may have started in the womb while she and my dad plotted their exit from the cult that they had given all of their possessions to, and through her traumatic experience of my birth. I entered the world a healthy ten pounds seven and a half ounces, breathing in the warm humid air of the southern bayous of New Orleans. Founded in the 1700s and later rebuilt in 1939 a few blocks from where the Superdome now stands, Charity Hospital was a teaching facility that was condemned and decommissioned after Hurricane Katrina. During my birth, nurses refused to allow my father in the room and restrained my mother while a row of obstetrical residents stood bedside and watched as the attending physician explained each step of the process.

By the time I had reached the third grade, I was racked with anxiety from talk of war. In the late 1970s, the dinner conversations frequently revolved around the Cold War or my dad's reminiscences about his time in Vietnam. Dad had been drafted into the war, but fate allowed him an office job working as a draftsman for the officers. Still, war terrified me. War and death were topics I could not grasp, yet they frightened me. I was afraid of losing my parents or my sister, Miranda, and of dying myself. I was sensing and absorbing information that was far beyond my comprehension, but I understood the gravity of it.

We lived in the path between the now decommissioned K. I. Sawyer Air Force Base in Marquette and an Air National Guard base in Battle Creek. As fighter jets roared overhead, I would press my scrawny back against the house to hide beneath the eaves, hoping the pilots could not see me on their training missions. There were several times when I was upstairs that the F-15s flew so low I could make out the pilots' masks. I would quickly duck to the floor, convinced they would crash through my bedroom window.

Between navigating my fear of death and conflict and the endless farm chores, I took refuge in reading every book about nature I could find. I drew elaborate underwater seascapes, dreaming of one day exploring the deep like my hero, Jacques Cousteau. The remote location of our little subsistence farm meant that playing with friends was seldom an option. Instead, I relied on my imagination to keep me occupied.

As much as my imagination was a source of entertainment and adventure on our remote homestead, my overactive mind could turn the unknown into a source of crippling fear. I was also extremely shy, which continued into my teenage years, often leading me to avoid answering the phone, afraid to engage with another human being. This was upsetting to my mom, especially when I hesitated to answer calls that were important, like when my dad hurt himself at work and needed to go to urgent care. This was one of the few times I heard my mom curse, and I was directly in the path of her angry outburst.

My mom was the youngest of three girls, with many years separating her from her older sisters. Her parents were extraordinarily strict Germans who never tolerated any disagreement from their children. They were quick to remind her that she was an accident and that they had wanted a boy instead. I ponder at times whether my mom feels that she is deserving of love. "Do as I say and don't question me" was their method of communication, and my mom carried this with her as she raised my sister and me. As I grew older I began to question and disagree with her, and she often would become silent and get teary, a defense mechanism she had used to avoid confrontation since I was a small child.

From my own experiences in hospitals, I can only imagine how cold and lonely my birth must have been for my mother, strapped to the bed and racked with contractions while pushing me into the world. With such an unceremonious entrance into life, it's no surprise that I seemed to feel the heaviness of the world too early. I suffered from scoliosis and poor posture and often wonder if that was a result of trying to hide, a result of my shyness and my fear of being seen. My slight frame buckled under the weight of it all.

By age eight, I had severe chest pains, a tightness between my intercostal muscles that was so intense that I found myself in the doctor's office several times. At each visit, the doctor shrugged off my symptoms, and the anxiety that gripped me even at that young age was never diagnosed.

I was afraid I would disappoint my parents; terrified my peers would reject me for wearing secondhand clothes, being too skinny, or being a nerd or a band geek; and worried my classmates would tease me for not knowing enough about pop culture or TV shows. I was also afraid of crying in front of the other kids and having them see how sensitive I was.

"Boys don't cry" is all I remember my fifth-grade teacher saying after I broke down in class for the third time that day.

To me, depression is a series of seemingly continuous obstacles inhibiting the ease I strive for. I am not sure when exactly depression first draped its heavy veil over my young mind, but it stole away those precious moments of childish wonderment. There is a moment late in childhood when our innocence is lost forever; mine came far too early. I only realized this years later when thumbing through photographs of my childhood. There was toddler Ben, blue eyes wide with curiosity and bright with innocent joy. Then, around age five, those eyes began to hold a heaviness and an awareness of death, of anger and pain, a knowledge that we are all going to die or, worse yet, go to hell.

Some say childlike wonder, that full immersion in the present moment, is similar to what adults who are under the influence of psychedelics experience. All of our left-brained anxiety and worry, the fear of not belonging or not measuring up, the concern that others may not like us, the disconnect we feel as adults are replaced in those moments with a sense of self-acceptance and connection to other beings. This is a feeling dogs have mastered, somehow staying in each moment while leaning in to offer support without a trace of judgment. That is, unless they have not had their daily adventure outside.

I am still unsure whether my childhood depression was due to the serotonin imbalance that seems to run in my immediate family, or the overwhelming flood of emotional stimuli that comes with a highly perceptive mind.

As I grew older, I dealt with the usual teenage angst and hormones and also grappled with obsessive-compulsive habits, going through odd routines of counting steps, turning lights on and off, and repeating phrases or little actions until I felt I had some control of my situation.

We lived in a remote area, so there were never really opportunities for me to get away with much outside of my mother's scrutiny. There was no texting or social media. I would have to agonize over a hand-written note, or use my family's rotary telephone to call a girl I had a crush on.

Sneaking out to faraway parties was nearly impossible, and since all of my friends at school had long-distance phone numbers, my mom would comb through the phone bills for any unfamiliar numbers and long-distance charges and ask me if they were calls to girls. Even though I would use a very long cord and drag the phone into my bedroom, I had to whisper into the phone so she could not hear me talking.

These aspects of my childhood left me ill prepared to navigate a society where most young people were able to date in junior high and high school. My mother was afraid I might meet a girl who would be a bad influence and sway me from our beliefs. She would question me constantly, as if my talking on the phone to a girl might get her pregnant.

While my peers seemed resigned to the limitations of small-town living, I always felt restless, knowing there was more to life than I had experienced in my sheltered upbringing. Early on, the woods felt so immense to me, but I always knew there was far more to explore beyond my backyard.

My mind is wired in such a way that I constantly analyze my environment, observing others' emotions while contemplating my own feelings and getting stuck in my head until I know enough to act. Sometimes the difficulty of expressing my feelings to other humans in the moment leaves me anxious and paralyzed. Those swirling feelings are calmed by simply stroking my pup's ears. I love the way dogs offer love and support without needing to question me before I have an answer, and their soothing sighs of contentment. Pressing my head against my dog's head and sharing a quiet moment of just breathing is one of the most grounding and centering acts for me. Stopping for this quiet moment to simply breathe and connect with a being that loves you equally always shifts the course of a day that previously felt overwhelming and haphazard.

This deep connection with my animal companions began in childhood. There was Justus, the gentle border collie mix who was my family's first dog; Jasper, a svelte mackerel tabby cat who survived years in the forest, multiple moves, and urban battles with alley cats twice his size; and Chassie, a fun- and food-loving black Labrador retriever. Despite being a shy and sensitive child who was terrified of answering the phone into my late teens, I felt at ease romping through the forest behind our house with Justus or Chassie. Dogs are masters of empathy and nonverbal communication, and I was able to let go of my anxiety and shyness with my canine (and feline) companions, exploring the forest and pretending I was Luke Skywalker or a great woodsman.

Justus was more of an outdoor dog, and his presence made me feel safe on our remote wooded property. Our home was far from our neighbors, and without consistent options for playmates, I quickly learned to value the companionship of dogs. I appreciated Justus's company, and with him at my side, my mother would allow me to play outdoors unsupervised, in search of treasure in the rows of pine trees and creeks that wound through the forest.

We lived a quarter mile off a rural dirt road, and during the harsh Michigan winters the driveway was impassable, especially for our rusty two-wheel-drive Chevy Blazer. My dad would use an old Ski-Doo snowmobile to pull me and my younger sister, Miranda, to the house in a modified toboggan, the sides built up to accommodate groceries and laundry and any other supplies for our off-grid abode.

Along the drive was an area where old appliances and building materials had been dumped, a common sight in the rural area around where I grew up. I was walking home on a warm and dry September day after the school bus dropped me off, and was halted by a wall of smoke billowing from the dump, the blackness covering the driveway. I tried to crawl under the smoke so I could get home to tell my mom that the dump was on fire. The smoke was so dense that it was impossible to get through, and, in a panic, I realized I would need to find a new route home. Sprinting through the woods, I searched for a trail or a familiar landmark. Overhead, I noticed a small plane circling, and felt my chest tense up. I wished Justus were there to lead me back and protect me from this new threat above. In tears, I tried to stay out of sight under the canopy of the trees, not realizing it was a forest service plane sent to keep an eye on the fire. Finally, I found myself in our backyard, and, hugging Justus, I told my mom in between sobs, "The dump is on fire! A plane is following me! They followed me all the way home!"

When Justus was in his later years, a friend of the family was raising a litter of puppies. Feeling the pull of the strong kinship I had always known with dogs, I wanted desperately to bring a puppy home. I begged my parents to keep one, but they told me that we could not adopt a second dog while Justus was still alive.

After Justus passed, a woman who worked with my dad on a log home–building crew offered us a black Lab puppy, and I was beside myself with joy. Chassie, with her fun-loving personality and soft floppy ears, gave me someone to hang out with during my awkward early teen years as I built forts deep within the forest behind our house, searching for the perfect white oak or pine trees for climbing. She was considered a part of the family and was allowed indoors. I felt safer in the presence of dogs, and, thankfully, she was always by my side.

Around that time, when I was twelve years old, my family took a vacation to Washington, DC, to visit my aunt. It was the first time I had experienced a big city, and as we toured the historic sites and museums, I wanted to document the awe I felt. Borrowing my mom's point-and-shoot camera, I captured my first-ever photographs on tiny 110 film, each frame measuring only sixteen millimeters across. I was so fascinated by the prints from that trip that I submitted my first photo to a *Parade* magazine photo contest. Later, I was hesitant to enroll in photography classes at my high school, fearing it would be too expensive and a stress on the tight budget my family lived on. My exposure to photography was limited to *National Geographic* and *Life* magazines, as well as the nature books I obsessed over.

Unfortunately, there were no photographers in my family to mentor me, but Mom documented our family well with her solid grasp of composition. My dad had an innate editorial eye, and the snapshots of his time in Vietnam always drew me into what he had experienced there.

A family friend named Ernie noticed my interest in photography and gave me a 100 series medium-format Polaroid. Although I never got it to work, I often got it out and imagined I was a photographer. I still have that camera today.

Although my animal friends were wonderful companions, what I craved deeply was human camaraderie. While in school, I longed for the acceptance that comes with being part of a team. My mom also forbade me from playing team sports in junior high, so instead I focused on reading books and practicing the trumpet for the school band, which I participated in from fifth to tenth grade. I was unaware of my athletic abilities prior to the eleventh grade, when I finally convinced my mom to let me run cross-country. Through distance running I learned how to push my body and mind through pain and discomfort. This newfound inner strength gave me more confidence within my own skin after years of being the scrawny Napoleon Dynamite nerd getting constantly picked on and knocked down by the football players and teased for being different.

Predictably, I got all of that out of my system in the first half of my freshman year of college with six months of repression-fueled partying. But after that, I hated how my body felt, and at the suggestion of Sheri G, the dorm roommate of my very first college friend, I tried out for the novice crew on the collegiate rowing team.

As a child, I had wanted more than anything to be socially accepted, to be part of a community, and to be good enough at something to be recognized as special. Crew fulfilled all those needs. Later, with Denali at my side, I would find a similar sense of community and confidence through rock climbing, photography, and surfing.

Rowing is grueling, one of the most difficult full-body workouts in all of athletics. A sprint race is two thousand meters and takes just under six minutes for a faster crew. After the first five hundred meters you hit the anaerobic threshold, then back off just as you're about to explode, hold that for four minutes of intense pain and lactic acid, and then ramp it up again for the last five hundred meters, timing the final stroke across the finish line with your collapse. All of this is done while focusing on syncing perfectly with the other members in the boat.

Yet when flow state, that magical swing, is attained, suddenly the shell seems to launch forward with a mind of its own. Breaths come easier, and blood flows back into your oxygen-deficient legs as the timing locks in with rare unison.

Our crew did not have a budget to fly to regattas, so we would pile into large passenger vans for each race, driving anywhere from three to fifteen hours. These weekly road trips also sparked my love for the open road and seeing people and places beyond the landscape I was raised in.

During my final season, my coach let me borrow his single, a gorgeous hand-built wooden Stämpfli racing shell made in Switzerland, to enter a head race, a four-thousand-meter time trial–type event where the only real opponent is oneself. The race was hosted by the Ohio State University and had a solid field of competitors, many of whom I knew well from the University of Michigan because of our frequent competitions with Big Ten teams. As I warmed up by paddling upstream toward the starting line, I began to hear hecklers on the shore and in other shells. I realized they were making fun of my boat, a beautiful piece of art with its wooden craftsmanship and matching wooden oars. All the other racers had cutting-edge carbon fiber shells and oars, and mine looked like a vintage relic.

I tried to shrug them off, focusing on my balance and the twinge coming from a recent hamstring injury. Both the pain and teasing helped take the pressure off, and I had few expectations since this was the biggest race I had ever entered solo. During the entire duration of the twenty-minute race, I pushed as hard as I could without aggravating my injury and focused only on overtaking the two racers ahead of me. I relished the feeling of independence and how responsive my coach's boat felt to every ounce of energy I put into propelling it forward.

An hour after the finish, I was standing on the shore with my teammates watching another event when the announcer began reading off the results of the top five finishers. I tried not to get my hopes up as he said the times for fifth place, then fourth . . . Finally he was at first and said, "Ben Moon, Grand Valley State University." I was stunned. How was that possible? I was forty-five seconds faster than second place against almost fifty competitors. Our coach, Richard Laurance, beamed as he quipped, "It was the boat, you know it was my boat!" This same mental focus and intuition is what got me through cancer, challenging film projects, and every life obstacle since.

My senior year, our team was very fast. It was the 1997 season, and our men's crew shared a special chemistry. None of us were particularly physically gifted or had any previous rowing experience, and we were tiny by heavyweight rower standards, averaging six feet one inch tall and 182 pounds. We were underdogs in every sense of the word.

Coach Laurance marveled at how eight smaller guys from a modest public university with a little-known rowing program won every Varsity 8 race we entered until the championship at the end of the season. We competed head-to-head with Big Ten and Ivy League schools, matching up with scholarship and national team rowers, all the way to the medal podium and grand finals at the most prestigious collegiate regattas in the country.

Four years of racing and training expanded my mental breaking point, my X factor, far beyond any pain threshold I could have imagined. Rowing transformed the 145-pound frame of a scrawny teenage boy into a V-shaped 180-pound man with huge lats and shoulders. I now have a thirty-inch waist, but when I was rowing, I had to wear size 34 jeans to accommodate my glutes and thighs, made muscular by the five to seven hours of daily training. I learned how to push myself beyond my mental and physical barriers for the other guys in my eight-man shell. No letting up, lest I let the others down. Not only did I fit into this community, I felt needed.

Rowing was a way for me not only to release all of the anxiety in my body, but also to focus my energy on something outside myself. My body strengthened, my scoliosis became nearly unnoticeable, and I was finally able to get out of my head. With every stroke, I let out the fear and paralysis I had felt growing up. My rowing years also encouraged me to pull up my Michigan roots and make the move out west, a choice that introduced me to Denali. That friendship would continue to foster my growth in my journey to manhood, giving me confidence to venture out into the unknown.

———

AFTER MY SERENDIPITOUS MEETING WITH DENALI, THE SHELTER ATTENDANT informed me that they needed to consider their decision overnight. The next day I felt even more strongly that Denali was a good fit. Melanie was at work, so I drove back to the shelter alone, signing the adoption paperwork while assuring the attendant that I had a dog-friendly home. *Oh crap,* I thought. *What will I tell my landlord?* I was quite aware that our lease explicitly prohibited dogs, but I quickly justified the decision to myself. *There is no way I can deny what I feel for*

*this furry little pup . . . he belongs in my life, and that is the one thing I'm
sure of. I'll figure out the details later.*

He sat nobly in my lap as I drove home, looking up at me.

> Thank you. You seem nice. Please don't abandon me like
> the last human did, okay? I'll love you forever. Please don't
> bring me back to that awful place! It's so loud and scary.

As he leaned back into my chest, my heart swelled with emotion.
I felt the beginnings of a rare friendship, the kind that defies explanation and somehow feels just right. Little did I know how often I would
lean into that friendship in the years that would follow, and how I
would find his warm and constant support in return.

I named him Denali, for the great mountain in Alaska whose name
comes from the Koyukon word *Deenaalee*, meaning "the high one"; it
also represented the wildness I longed for within my own life.

2

New Beginnings

When Denali was three months old, I introduced him to the hallowed canyon walls of Smith Rock. At first Denali was confused by climbing. Why do you tie my leash to the tree roots at the base of the wall, then you tie into a different rope, and then you leave me down here? He would whimper and bark, trying to tell me I should come down. Eventually, he recognized that I always came back for him, and he would do the full body wag, excitedly welcoming me back to the ground. I hugged him, and as he licked every inch of my face, I dreamed that my other companion in life could be as happy as Denali was to see me.

Melanie and I were married seven months after we met. On a cold spring evening in Grand Haven amid the sandy backdrop of my favorite beach, I proposed to her in the dark. My motivations came from behind my heart, like I had someone pushing me between my shoulder blades and I was powerless to resist. I reasoned that it felt like the logical step in life that I had to move through. A saner foundation for marriage would have come from a place of undeniable love.

Melanie's family valued recreation and fun for fun's sake in the outdoors, something I had always yearned for. Instead of snowboarding, rock climbing, and mountain biking, my family focused their energies on necessity, making sure the vegetable garden flourished and the freezer was stocked with wild game. My dad was a conquistador of the useful and taught me how to hunt and fish and work hard, all life skills I now cherish, but we lacked the financial resources for ski trips or vacations in the tropics.

Melanie's mom heaped compliments upon me, and even though things were not going well, my deepest desire was for someone to affirm that I seemed to be on the right path. This encouragement of the relationship was unfamiliar, as my mother had not allowed me to date in high school.

I was finishing up an internship at the local hospital under the mentorship of the lead athletic trainer and an orthopedic surgeon overseeing the health of all the athletes at a nearby high school. My graduation from GVSU, athletic training board exams, twenty-third birthday, and wedding date all piled on their own stressors, and all were to happen over the course of a few weeks. I was having paralyzing anxiety attacks, and I had no idea what to do.

I made an appointment with the family doctor I had seen since I was a toddler, and shared my symptoms of being overwhelmed and having insomnia and chest pains. Without hesitation, he diagnosed my condition as anxiety and handed me a blister pack of antianxiety medication. Then, with Melanie sitting next to me and with the same frankness of delivery of a cancer diagnosis, he asked, "Are you sure that you're marrying the right person?"

I was too stunned by the boldness of the question to react. I laughed nervously and said, "Yes, of course!" to defuse the awkwardness that hung in the air. In the lead-up to the nuptials, my intuition was nearly always a cacophony of shrill warnings, but I was too bullheaded to heed them. I was going to get married come hell or high water, even though I was woefully lacking in experience with romantic relationships.

The wedding was held in the backyard of Melanie's childhood home with over a hundred in attendance. The support on my side of the aisle consisted of only my parents and sister, my best man, and a friend I had grown up with who had a crush on Melanie's younger sister.

I blame no one for my marrying the wrong person for reasons other than love, only my own stubborn naivete. I went along with the formalities like a head of cattle being herded through a stockyard.

After the wedding, I juggled my athletic training duties at the high school with a gig at an outdoor gear shop called Earth's Edge, a few blocks from Lake Michigan. Rock climbing, snowboarding, mountain biking, and backpacking were occupying most of my thoughts in those days. I was too excited about the freedom to pursue these newfound passions to turn any attention to the needs of my marriage.

Reading *Climbing* magazine, I was astonished by the breathtaking imagery of seemingly impossible climbs. I dreamed of one day attempting to climb in these locales. I had spent hours in climbing gyms and was ecstatic to have the opportunity to climb outdoors for the first time, testing my novice skills on a short overhanging climb at Devil's Lake in Wisconsin.

After reading a review of the best cameras to use while rock climbing, I felt an impulse to purchase my first film camera and ordered a Yashica T4 point and shoot. Little did I know then how important a role this creative curiosity would play.

The feeling of freedom I experienced while dancing up the vertical rock faces at Smith Rock was in drastic contrast to the other reality I was facing, the deterioration of my relationship with Melanie. The increasing frequency of our fights left me feeling trapped and lonely with a frustration I felt deep in my chest, a feeling that I was losing control. All I could think about was climbing and living the life I didn't know how to manifest but knew was out there. The finances grew tighter every day as I struggled to find job a that matched my recently completed degree in sports medicine. I searched all over town for work in my field, but I found only short-lived gigs as a personal trainer in dank fitness centers, positions for which I was vastly overqualified after the thousands of hours I had put into working with athletes.

I began teaching climbing at a cutting-edge climbing gym, but it was tied to a corporate fitness facility, and I was required to wear a white Adidas polo while I hung from a rope setting climbing routes on the wall. Men were also not allowed to remove our shirts while climbing, no matter how hot and sweaty the gym got. Everything felt controlled, and it stifled my spirit.

A restlessness welled up as I became acutely aware that suburban life simply did not suit me. The frustration of working jobs beneath my skill set pushed me to fall back on the building projects that I had helped my dad with as a teenager, and I began framing houses for a local builder.

The Pacific Northwest winter did little to lift my mood, and Denali's distaste for the incessant Portland rain seemed even stronger than mine. He would refuse to go outside until his bladder absolutely could not hold on any longer. If the grass was muddy, he'd lean toward it with two paws on the sidewalk, the other two barely touching the grass, and take a leak into the lawn with only minimal contact with the mucky soil. It was as if he wanted to avoid prolonged contact with the dampness lest he imply that he actually enjoyed the wet climate. Denali's distaste for the rain matched his unease in the city, yet he would come to life once we pulled into our high-desert camp for a weekend of climbing at Smith.

Denali matured quickly, and around nine months of age he began to develop the confidence to become a more adventurous crag dog. I was invited on a trip to the Needles, a picturesque granite mecca just south of Yosemite Valley in the Sierra Nevada. The crew included the legendary climbers Tony Yaniro and Sue Nott, and renowned rock climbing photographer Jim Thornburg. Each day, in order to get to the granite spires where the climbs were located, we made the four-mile uphill approach. The last mile had some scrambling over granite boulders that seemed to intimidate young Denali. Hesitant and crying at first, he eventually realized it was quicker to just learn how to overcome each obstacle than be lifted over them.

This was my first time really testing my knee on climbs after an ACL repair surgery, and also my final trip with Melanie before things really fell apart. I became frustrated over petty things on that trip, and we bickered regularly. I was distracted by the beauty of the perfect granite climbs, learning from Tony, following the climbing master up pitch after pitch of perfect granite cracks. Jim Thornburg asked to take my photo on a spooky arête—basically a 150-foot corner of a building that lacked any real handholds. I grimaced my way up the climb while Jim snapped image after image. One of them ended up as a full-page image in *Climbing*. Little did I realize then how much Jim's work and that trip would influence my own career in photography.

One evening back in camp, I was looking for Denali when I realized he had crawled into our tent. *Wait, wasn't the door zipped closed? I always shut it to keep the mosquitoes out*, I thought.

I looked closer and realized Denali had used his claws to slice through the screen door of the tent.

A black Lab in our camp had been bullying Denali, so he crawled in to hide in the safest and most convenient place he could find. The mosquitoes found me eventually.

Upon our return to the city, I felt daily life grinding my morale to its lowest depths. The stress of finding a job in an overwhelming city, balancing the finances when money seemed to never be quite enough, and never truly connecting with and loving my partner broke me.

The bickering between Melanie and me dragged us both down. Tempers flared and both of us began to wander, Melanie in action, and me in my imagination. We both worked at the climbing gym, and Melanie began falling for one of the facility's employees, a tall, long-haired front desk clerk named Brody. I was no match for his smooth lies and easy charm, and it is no wonder Melanie was caught up in the fantasy of a man who tempted her with every quality she felt I was incapable of offering.

Even when Denali was a puppy, he would mirror my moods. Ever observant and in tune, he acted upon his anxiousness about the situation between Mel and me by gnawing on baseboards and shredding baskets in our apartment while Mel and I were at work. Denali could clearly see the dysfunction of the marriage, but I was so close to it all that my anxiety blinded me to reading the signs.

I dreamed of a woman who could understand me, to shine past my darkness and bring hope into my heart. I realize now that happiness starts within, that we alone are accountable for our actions. Yet a loving touch or a well-timed word of encouragement can forever alter our life's course. In those lonely moments when I felt misunderstood and unseen, Denali's presence helped me stay grounded. No matter how bad I felt about the constant bickering or how the weather and business of the city life brought me down, one trip over the mountains to Smith Rock or to the beach would bring me back to feeling human again. Denali would go from being apathetic and anxious in the city to a playful and enthusiastic companion amid the expanse of the high desert or Oregon coast.

Melanie was the rescuer for her family. She would often fly home to care for her dad during his separations from her mother, for her little brother whenever he grappled with mental illness, and for her sister when she battled eating disorders. As an EMT, she was there when a man crumpled to the ground from a heart attack. I often wondered why in my own struggles with depression, she never was able to connect with me or make much of an attempt to help me in my distress. Instead, Melanie would belittle me and make me feel inadequate for the challenges I faced without the resources to overcome them.

Her lack of empathy for my condition made me feel unseen and misunderstood, and in frustration I would raise my voice. As I waited for Melanie to respond, a feeling that I was detached from my body would overcome me. I would retreat inward, curling up within my mind. I learned this defense mechanism early on when my mom took away my ability to choose for myself. There, in the confines of my solitary headspace, I would faintly hear Melanie berating me for not being able to find a job in my field.

While these salvos whistled overhead, Denali would curl up nearby, observing from the perimeter and making sure I was okay. His presence made the space feel safe, like Justus had once done as we explored the woods during my childhood. Denali was definitely a male dog, a dude who couldn't always show his emotions. His husky aloofness added to this veneer. Yet he always drew me outward, into the outdoors, toward moving my body and climbing. This pulled me out of the confusion and anxiety that swirled in my head, offering a brief respite from the emotional turmoil that consumed the household.

I struggled to make sense of my life, which seemed to be a ship that I was no longer captain of. I kept the books on our finances, and I would scrutinize each purchase as I attempted to manage concrete variables that were within my ability to control. To Melanie's frustration, I would disagree with purchases that I deemed frivolous, even though it might be an item she felt she needed. After she asked if we could afford to replace her running shoes and I said no, I overheard her make a spiteful remark to a climbing gym patron: "I need new ones, but Ben won't let me buy a new pair."

Later, when I bought my first "real" camera setup that cost around a thousand dollars, she was furious. The camera I purchased was a used Nikon N90s film body, and two fast zoom lenses. Melanie was horrified by the expense, and it seemed to reinforce her opinion that I was selfish, but in hindsight, it seems that my subconscious survival instincts had awoken my creative desires to prepare me for an unexpected new path. I bought the kit from Pro Photo Supply in Portland the very same week that I discovered Melanie's relationship with Brody had become intimate.

My only photography lesson was an hour-long photo walk that same week with my friend Matt Menely. He had gone to photography school and had published images of Tommy Caldwell and other climbers, and I was eager to learn from him. When I was making my purchase at Pro Photo, I called Matt to ask his recommendations for lenses to start out with. He showed me how to use my camera's settings to expose my images properly, lessons I carried with me through the years as I honed my craft. The first image I shot on slide film was of the Union Station tower from the Broadway Bridge. Every time I biked over that bridge in the years following, I was reminded of these humble sparks that serendipitously caught fire just as my relationship burned to the ground.

After the lesson with Matt was completed, I wandered into Pioneer Square, where a pro-Gore, anti-Bush rally was taking place. It was November 2000, and Portlanders were livid over the infamous presidential election recount. I snapped a few images of the demonstrations and developed the Provia print film on the commute back to Beaverton. Excited about my work, I proudly showed the photos to Melanie. She was not impressed, and her lack of enthusiasm for my newfound passion crushed me.

That same evening, I was still buzzing with excitement from my first taste of photography until after dinner. Melanie then slid me a handwritten note across the table. I began to read it, realizing she had listed all of her needs that I had not met during the relationship. It felt a bit ironic that she had never communicated these needs in the moment and was only doing so now when she was already headed out the door. As I read through the note, I fought back tears and felt like a complete failure. Melanie then delivered the final blow. She told me that she had often faked her orgasms, twisting the knife already buried in my gut.

As I sat in stunned silence, Denali began to pant noisily as he lay against my leg. I glanced down and realized he felt every bit of my pain. *Thank you, friend. Please don't take it on*, I thought. *I just wish you could take it all away.*

> I can! Please let me. We just have to leave this place.
> I'm here for you, friend.

Over the course of the summer, Melanie and I had been planning a climbing road trip to the eastern Sierra Nevada, followed by a move to the high-desert recreation town of Bend. Bend is a mellow city known for the Deschutes River that winds through its core with easy access to snowboarding, mountain biking, rock climbing, white-water kayaking, and nearly every outdoor activity short of surfing, and I hoped we could make a fresh start there. In anticipation of the journey, I had quit my construction job, excited about the road trip and the new life that lay ahead. My parents were visiting from Michigan for the Thanksgiving holiday, so with the help of Miranda and her boyfriend, who lived in Portland, we moved all of our marital possessions into a storage locker in Bend. Denali had been acting listless the entire day, and I assumed he was nervous after seeing all of the packing up that was going on. But when Denali began to vomit and have diarrhea, I did not yet realize that his intuition that a cyclone loomed on the horizon was the cause of his sudden illness.

The evening of the big move, Melanie dropped me off at the apartment and told me she was going to stay at Brody's that night. Reflexively, I ripped the wedding band off my finger and yelled, "Whatever that thing means!" and flung it at the dashboard of our Subaru.

Melanie stumbled into our bedroom somewhere around four a.m.

reeking of booze, and she revealed that she had been making out with Brody. Whether it was simply a confession or of vengeful intent, her words made me physically ill, and I rushed to the toilet and began to vomit uncontrollably. Denali was out of sorts as well, following close behind me into the bathroom. He looked at me with helplessness as I heaved into the toilet bowl.

> Hey, man, how can I help? This feels so awful. I feel sick too. Here, let me try this . . .

Denali licked my hand, then just went for it and licked my vomit-stained face. And then, leaning his body weight into me, he slid down to a lying position at my side.

To avoid confrontation, Melanie took the car and disappeared while my parents were at a Sunday morning Bible meeting, after I had told them I was too sick to come along, and stayed away for the rest of Thanksgiving weekend. With my family gathered around, my mom asked where Melanie had gone. I had to break the news to my parents—and finally myself—that Melanie was seeing someone else.

I recognize now that if she had shared the things on her list with me earlier, I might not have had the maturity or the capacity to absorb them, or the ability to change without the aid of outside counseling.

Because all of our stuff had been moved to Bend in anticipation of the road trip I had been looking forward to for months, everything we owned was in storage except for two large North Face duffel bags, a bouldering crash mat, and a bin full of our food and cooking supplies. I hoped that somehow we could just leave on the trip and this night-mare would all be a silly dream. These hopes evaporated on the Tuesday following Thanksgiving. I came home from a long, rainy slog at the construction framing job site to find a note in place of Melanie's duffel informing me that she had left and that it was over between us.

As much as I had sensed the imminence of her departure, the void I felt upon it becoming a reality shook me to my core. I'd grown up in a deeply religious and conservative family where marriage was unquestionably a lifelong commitment, with divorce looked upon as the ultimate failure.

Reeling but pragmatic, I quickly signed a lease for an apartment nearby, hopeful that I could make amends with Melanie there. My apartment bordered the Sunset Highway, an east-to-west artery connecting the metropolis of Portland with the Coast Ranges, the gateway to the Pacific Ocean. Within the unassuming suburban complex, the decor of my new living space was that of a typical one-bedroom apartment, complete with beige carpets, off-white walls, and a gas fireplace. It was a place where I could shed anonymous tears while I searched to regain my sense of center.

I attempted to settle into the sparse layout with my few possessions. Denali's food and water bowl sat on the linoleum kitchen floor alongside his hand-sewn leash made from a climbing sling and Denali's favorite pieces of equipment: a ball thrower and a tattered tennis ball. Denali and I lounged on a foldout nylon camp couch that, along with my now-archaic desktop computer with its CRT monitor, made the living room look awkwardly spacious. We slept on an improvised mattress from a small thirty-by-forty-eight-inch bouldering crash pad meant for climbing. Sleep was impossible to find, and every night, holding Denali tight to my chest, I shed a stream of tears and grappled with the gut-wrenching betrayal and shame-filled guilt of what might have been.

As I overpowered the aloofness of Denali's husky side with tight hugs and coaxed his pit bull tendencies for closeness, he became an expert at snuggling during those endless tear-filled nights. Through my numbness and confusion, I found him to be the friend I could share my raw emotions with as I struggled to make sense of this new and frightening reality. The American dream of a marriage, a house, and family that had been until only recently my obvious road map was now a hollow promise filled with dead-end detours and decommissioned highways. "It's just you and me, Denali," I would whisper. "Just you and me."

I have always been a problem solver, and these drastic circumstances motivated me to search for solutions. Melanie complied with my request to meet and chat at my new apartment, and as she sat at the Formica bar, she made a subtly condescending remark. "This place is nice . . . ," she said. Meaning "how in the world did you afford this on your own?" My attempt at a romantic and expensive sushi dinner followed, and the result was just as fruitless.

I read countless relationship and self-help books after Melanie left, hoping to make sense of what had happened. It was easy to blame her for the infidelity, and these books confirmed for me that she was in the wrong. I felt shame and guilt for the failure of the marriage, but I was too shocked to look in the mirror and realize my part in pushing Melanie away.

I photocopied pages of the self-help books that I felt proved Mel's actions were wrong, hoping she would read them. My desperation made my attempts pathetic—somehow I hoped my "diagnosis" of her motivations for the affair with Brody would miraculously change her mind, yet when she dismissed my attempts with disdain I wasn't surprised.

Melanie suggested an appointment with a couple's therapist, kindling a flicker of hope. This was extinguished in the first session. It seemed her motivation was simply to incite me to have a yelling tantrum, hoping an angry outburst from me could justify her actions. To my face, she told me that yes, she had indeed been sleeping with Brody.

I listened quietly and attempted to absorb the unsurprising but still-excruciating news. "Thank you for telling me," I said, surprised at how strong and calm my voice felt. Startled, she looked at me, expecting me to explode in frustration. Instead, I slowly inhaled and nodded. Inside, my stomach raged with a heat that tore me apart after her admission of what I already knew.

The purpose of our second session was to tell me that she wanted out, was not coming back, and wanted a divorce. The counseling was simply a safe place for her to tell me what she wanted and what she had done, but there was zero opportunity for my input, much less any hope of reconciliation.

The following week, Melanie casually asked for the keys to the storage unit in Bend, mentioning that she just wanted to grab a few clothes and things. I immediately suspected she was not telling the whole truth, so I asked if she wanted to take Denali along with her on the trip, knowing that he would have my back.

My intuition was soon proved correct when Melanie asked if I could come to pick up a box of my things she had accidently grabbed from storage. I stopped by her apartment and was stunned as I surveyed the room. I could see every piece of our furniture in her place, including our bed, through an open door down the hall. Every item she had considered hers was there, yet the place felt strangely staged.

After peeking into her empty and unused fridge, I realized the whole rental was a front, and I surmised that she had been staying at Brody's all along.

Melanie continued toward the exit. Any efforts to reconcile were no match for what she was finding in her new romance with Brody. My constant attempts to show that I could change were only met with contempt, and I slowly began to recognize that Melanie's image of me in no way resembled the man I knew I was.

After several more disheartening attempts to win her back, I gathered my remaining shreds of dignity and accepted the futility of the task. Within the haze of pain and confusion, I glanced inward, and saw for the first time with remarkable clarity the depression I had grappled with for so much of my life.

I was driving to teach a rock climbing clinic and caught a blurb on National Public Radio advertising a clinical trial for depression at Oregon Health and Science University, a prestigious teaching hospital where four years later I would have my cancerous tumor staged. I nervously called the number and was soon enrolled in the test study. During the consult the staff told me that it was a trial studying the efficacy of endorphins to combat mental illness. I shared with the psychiatrist that in college I had found that rowing on the crew team was a big help in keeping negativity at bay. He told me that I was most likely just situationally depressed from the separation with Melanie, and I agreed that this was indeed a difficult time. Resolute to find a solution, I elaborated on my childhood and that I had grappled with anxiety and depression since I was young.

I shared with him that I had been consumed with fears of nuclear annihilation when I was five during the Cold War days, that I had severe chest pains due to anxiety at age eleven, and that I had grappled with fairly severe obsessive-compulsive disorder throughout my teens.

I informed him that both of my parents were on low doses of Zoloft. I recognized that mental illness was a red flag and a preexisting condition for insurance companies, and told him I was hesitant to get on antidepressants for that reason. He told me that he was not going to enroll me in the study and prescribed a regimen of Zoloft. "You can fill this if you like," he said. "I think it would help you at least get through this spell with your ex." Instead, my mom asked our family doctor to up her dose, and for four years she cut her pills in two, sharing the halves with me so I could take the drug without it ever appearing on my medical charts.

Once I got over feeling guilty about these new and unfamiliar feelings of "happiness," the antidepressants helped me return to life. To those not suffering from depression, this happy feeling was closer to a baseline "normal" mood, but to me it was novel. Far more powerful than any pharmaceutical, however, was the lift I got by simply stroking Denali's ears and seeing his loving response. A study by University of Missouri scientists has since shown that petting dogs causes a spike in a person's serotonin levels, the same neurotransmitter that my antidepressants were affecting. With the potent combination of medication and Denali's steady friendship, I gradually pulled myself out of the depths and started to move beyond simple survival. I began to feel the spark of life again.

I asked for my construction job back, and my boss let me start immediately. He clearly saw what I was going through, and I appreciated that he did not ask for details. In spite of not using my college degree, I appreciated that I could bring Denali with me to work every day. He would hang out in the back of the Subaru wagon on his bed, with the hatch open. Often, I would let him roam around the job site if we were in an area with less traffic.

Denali met his first cat around that time on a job site in the Coast Ranges. I held Denali close to the kitten, letting him sniff the little fur ball. Instead of an amicable greeting, the kitten swatted his nose, drawing blood. The kitten sprinted off and Denali gave chase, beginning his lifelong mission to eat at least one cat. He never was successful, but he certainly tried.

Later, he broke his pinkie toe chasing a chipmunk through a rock pile. At the veterinary office a huge cat was caged in the hallway, and as we passed, a paw emerged from inside, swinging at Denali. He yelped in pain, and I saw the cat had left a full claw buried in Denali's nose. Cats constantly reinforced the notion that they were out to harm him, so the best solution was for him to chase them away.

Around the time I asked for my construction job back, I had also begun teaching rock climbing in the evenings at the Nike World Headquarters in Beaverton in a building known to employees as the "Lance" before Nike dropped him after Armstrong admitted to doping during his career. I was working hard on my own climbing as a reprieve from the emotional pain I felt. I soon "sent" the hardest route I had climbed up to this point in time, a steep and athletic sport climb called Aggro Monkey. The route was rated 5.13b, a grade that represented its advanced difficulty level within the American grading protocol for hikes and climbs, also known as the Yosemite Decimal System. At the time, 5.14d was considered the hardest route in the world.

The climb was located up in a rocky gully at Smith Rock, where a dedicated crew of local and traveling climbers would congregate to test their physical and mental endurance. As I tied in for each attempt, Denali would nuzzle up next to me, helping to calm my nerves as I carefully strapped on my shoes and chalked up my hands, preparing for the challenge that lay ahead on the wall. I often had doubts that I could actually climb the route, especially before I broke into sending a higher "number grade" of climbs, such as when I sent Aggro Monkey, my first 5.13 route. My hardest climb prior to that route had been a 5.12c, but Denali's calm presence helped me believe in my abilities and step out of what I thought was possible. As I started up the first moves of the climb, he would curl up at the base of the route. Pushing myself far beyond what I thought I could physically accomplish helped me clear out the mental chatter and was another immense step toward healing and feeling whole again.

My passion and rudimentary education in photography began in the lonely hours after Melanie left. I pored over how-to library books on photography and shot through countless rolls of Fuji Velvia and Kodak Tri-X film. My early photographs were awkward family shots, ill-composed landscapes, and close-ups of flowers.

A few months after my separation from Melanie, I was invited to join a bouldering trip to the Eastern Sierra of California, which John Muir once referred to as "the Range of Light" for the majestic landscapes and surreal quality of light. This experience both snapped me out of my heartbreak and reignited my interest in photography. The colors of the alpenglow playing on the granite Buttermilk Boulders, with the White Mountains on one side and the majestic Sierra Nevada on the other, had opened my mind to a whole new way of seeing the world.

Denali tolerated my request for him to pose, each slap of the shutter serving as an expensive teacher on my awkward photographic journey. He quickly recognized that if he was in front of the camera, all of my attention would be focused on him. After that discovery, it was hard for me to capture an image without Denali first sneaking into the frame.

Later that spring, I received word from Melanie that she had moved to West Virginia and was guiding white-water trips on the Gauley River. Now that saving the relationship was beyond question, my reasons for staying in Portland had dwindled to none. She had left all of our possessions behind in a storage unit and told me that I could have anything I wanted, I just needed to ask Brody for the key. To save further pain, I let that life and its possessions go and declined to take her up on that offer. I still have no idea what became of any of those things.

3

The Dirtbag Life

I ached for a life beyond the claustrophobic confines of Portland and began to put out feelers for work on the sunnier, drier side of the Cascade Range. On Friday morning I received a call confirming I had landed a gig in Bend, and by Sunday afternoon my sister, Miranda, and I had packed up the last of my few possessions as late-spring sunlight spilled in the windows, testing my intentions to leave the city. The air smelled fresh, even hopeful, as I packed my belongings neatly into the small cargo area of my Subaru wagon. By nightfall, every tiny space in the vehicle and the cargo box mounted on top had been utilized. Even the front passenger seat was stacked nearly to the height of my shoulder. Eager to depart, I asked Denali to load up, and he curled up on the driver's seat, wanting nothing to do with the cramped arrangement on the passenger side. I looked at Denali and scratched his head with both hands. Sensing my elation, he perked up and stood and wagged his tail. After a full-body shake, he crawled to the top of the pile and curled up again.

> Obviously you're excited to leave, and it must be for
> something fun, because I haven't seen you this happy
> in six months. Regardless of what's happening, there's
> no way you're leaving me behind, so I'll squeeze in . . .
> just this once.

Denali rode at eye level with me and let out a contented sigh as we merged onto Interstate 84 and drove east, the miles slowly separating us from Portland, my old life, and worries.

As the miles passed and the Sitka spruce and cloudy gloom gave way to ponderosa pines and a crisp high-desert sky filled with stars, a breathtaking sense of freedom welled up within me. Glancing over at Denali, I felt the heaviness lifting from my soul. I reached over to scratch his head lightly and he looked back, ears perked in anticipation. The air felt lighter, and Denali sensed a new adventure lay ahead . . . an adventure that would soon replace the burden of conflict and heartbreak he had borne over the past six months.

I whispered to Denali, "It's just you and me, my friend, just you and me."

That night, we slept on the ground under the stars at Skull Hollow, a primitive BLM campground known unofficially to climbers as the Grasslands. As I breathed in the scent of fresh growth on the sage bushes and juniper trees, I pictured days spent testing myself on the vertical walls of Smith Rock, just on the other side of the hill. I slept soundly with Denali at my side and awoke to air that smelled clean. My head felt clearer than it had in years. The realization began to settle that my path was shifting from the confusion I had grappled with to a life outdoors, filling our days with the adventures that I dreamed of for Denali and me.

And there, in the brisk morning air of the high desert, we began our new life together.

———

A COUPLE OF YEARS EARLIER WHILE TEACHING CLIMBING AT MY UNIVERSITY'S rock wall, I saw a Metolius climbing gear catalog that featured images of employees at work, with their dogs everywhere: lying at their feet, lounging under sewing tables, romping around in the machine shops, and hanging out at local climbing crags. Metolius seemed like an ideal place for a passionate climber and an adventurous dog like Denali to work, and the fact that dogs were welcome at all times meant that Denali and I would be able to spend our days together.

After the reality had set in that Melanie was not coming back, I put the word out to see if I could land a job there. Just weeks later, a friend who worked in customer service at Metolius called to let me know of an opening at their headquarters, located on the northern outskirts of the recreational mecca of Bend. After two long years enduring the dreary Portland rain, I knew any job in this high-desert paradise was too good to pass up.

I applied immediately and got the call to come down to the offices for an interview. I'm not sure there was much competition for the position, a production job in the cutting room where the harnesses, crash pads, slings, and big wall gear were prepped for the sewing floor. I didn't care how menial the position was—this was both the escape I had longed for and an opportunity to recast my identity while building a new life with Denali on my own terms. Adopting an active and outdoor-loving pup while still in the city had presented countless challenges and caused a lot of guilt when I sensed that he was feeling cooped up. Now we could work side by

side together in a workplace that encouraged adventure and after-
noons off.

————

I DUSTED OFF THE VOLCANIC DUST FROM MY SLEEPING PAD AND DOWN
sleeping bag, and carefully packed them back into the car. I did not
want to be late for my first day on the job, so I allowed an hour for the
drive south to the Metolius offices. Situated in view of the constant
north-south traffic of US 97, their factory is a cluster of rundown,
unassuming buildings next to a landscaping supply yard. Inside, amid
the racket of CNC machines grinding out the aluminum lobes for
camming devices—removable gear used for protection while ascending cracks in the rock—was a scene that resembled a cross between a
hippie commune and *Animal House.*

Each employee had their own key to the facilities, chose the number of hours they worked, and could come and go as they pleased,
provided they weren't holding up the production schedule. The sounds
of sewing and bar-tacking machines clattered away as a pack of dogs
gallivanted happily through the halls and aisles of the second-floor
sewing area. Denali looked uncertain at first, overwhelmed by the
stimulation coming from all sides. He looked up at me, and his tail
began to wag rapidly as he realized we were here to stay. Denali pranced
past the swirl of dogs and greeted each sewer at their station, nudging
their arms or sides to bring their attention to him. This is heaven, so
many people to love on me!

I worked as a cutter, a basic production job on the floor where
the soft goods were sewn. I was responsible for preparing each piece
of Dyneema and nylon webbing, polyester fabric, and foam padding

necessary to assemble climbing harnesses, chalk bags, bouldering crash pads, and slings and quickdraws used for sport climbing.

The easygoing community at Metolius and constant access to climbing outdoors helped me shift away from the feelings of guilt that still racked me over my separation with Melanie. She had moved out east without finalizing the legal side of our marriage. Instead of filing for divorce, she ghosted, leaving me to mop up the details. After dealing with the joint bank accounts, taxes, and car loans for months, I did my best to suppress all the voices in my head screaming, *Divorce is wrong. If you file for divorce, you didn't try hard enough and gave up too soon. Do you want to check the "divorced" status box on every questionnaire for the rest of your life? No woman will ever want to be with you if you're divorced.*

I walked into the county offices to fill out the paperwork. Fortunately, the only thing I owned of value was my well-used Subaru wagon and a bit of camping and climbing gear, so there was no battle over dividing of assets. Melanie let me keep my dog and the car, which is all I really wanted anyway. Losing Denali to the divorce would have been unimaginable, and fortunately because he had always been my companion, the subject never came up. After months of waiting for Melanie to complete the paperwork, I was relieved when the legal part of the divorce was completed. It would take over a decade for me to feel that same closure emotionally.

Unless you decide to only focus on bouldering, rock climbing can be an expensive pursuit. A major perk of working at Metolius was first dibs on deeply discounted climbing gear. Each evening, I would peruse the seconds bins after quality control inspected a round of cams prior to making them available for public sale. Each cam would retail

between $50 and $100, and a solid "trad rack"—an assortment of camming devices for crack climbing—spanned cracks of every size, from
smaller than a pinkie finger to the width of two fists stacked side by
side. This meant a minimum of ten cams were necessary to cover the
general range of sizes. For areas like Indian Creek in Utah with "splitter" parallel cracks that have little variance for the entire hundred-
foot-length of each "pitch" or half rope length, up to five cams in each
size are required. Building a solid rack could run anywhere from $500
to several thousands of dollars. With access to discounts, I could build
my rack for a tiny fraction of the retail cost. Because I was determined
to live cheaply and save money for camera gear and climbing trips,
Denali and I lived out of my Subaru wagon. We sometimes parked at
the Grasslands, but as many employees had done in the past, we most
often slept in the parking lot outside Metolius.

Denali gradually made friends with the other office dogs, loving
the easy freedom of roaming from one room to the next. He also developed a few rivalries. The worst was with Oliver, a dopey black Labrador and Newfoundland mix. He reminded me of a moose, with his
lanky legs that looked as if they could not possibly support his body
weight. He would chase Denali out of the room where the chalk bags
were sewn, then stand guard looking like a bit of a doofus with his
hilarious underbite and long, scrawny legs. One day I was standing
beside Maureen, the lead harness sewer, asking about a custom order,
when the back of my legs suddenly felt warm. I stepped forward, thinking I must be near a space heater. I felt a hot trickle down my leg and
glanced back only to see Ollie with his leg lifted, emptying his entire
bladder on the back of my legs. He looked elated as he dropped his leg
and awkwardly strutted way. "Oliver!" I hollered as Denali appeared

at my side. He sniffed my legs, and his tail and ears dropped when he recognized what had happened.

Oliver just claimed you?! Nooooo! How did this happen?

I ran down to the car to grab jeans to replace the urine-soaked pair I was wearing and headed back upstairs to look for Denali. I searched every room, unable to find him anywhere, until I saw a movement in one of the large cardboard boxes filled with scrap webbing. "There you are! Come on, buddy, let's go, I need a shower."

Denali refused to budge, looking away when I came closer. He was clearly sulking as he stared into the corner.

Why did you let him claim you? And of all the dogs, why Oliver? I can still smell him on you. Go away, I'm not moving from this box.

———

WHEN WINTER ARRIVED IN BEND THAT YEAR AND THICK LAYERS OF ICE formed on the inside of the car windows, I was determined to prove all my friends wrong who had doubted I would ever make it through a freezing cold central Oregon winter. Many nights I fell asleep fully clothed with long underwear and layers of fleece and puffy down jackets, shivering under the pile of blankets covering my down sleeping bag. Denali would often burrow beneath the layers and curl up next to me. I would spoon him to share body heat, a collective warm escape from the frigid air in our makeshift abode.

I often felt lost and unsure about what life held next, but Denali's stoic support helped me hold on to a hope of a new chapter just beyond the horizon. The tight quarters and lack of creature comforts were small sacrifices toward that goal, and Denali and I learned to adapt to the twenty-five-square-foot living space complete with towering three-foot ceilings. It was challenging to get dressed each day in a horizontal position, so Denali would scooch against the wheel well to allow me space to wriggle into my layers. If it was cold, we would snuggle up at night, and in the summer heat Denali and I would allow each other space to sprawl out.

One benefit of such a tiny living space was the motivation to spend nearly every waking hour outside exploring or rock climbing, taking the mornings slow to allow the temps to warm or drop depending on the season. This lifestyle suited Denali and me well. We were in this together, on an adventure that I hoped would last a very long time.

My work schedule at Metolius was anything but conventional, which allowed for long road trips and nine-day weekends if I planned it out just right. I often pushed the limits of the already-relaxed rules, cramming my allotted weekly hours into just a few days so Denali and I and could break free and explore, which usually meant climbing at Smith Rock or road trips south to my favorite climbing destinations.

I maintained a small storage unit just up the street from Metolius where I stored my belongings that wouldn't fit inside my little home or the storage box I kept on top as my "closet." I was working late one evening, as I often did after a full day of climbing at Smith Rock. I was cramming in hours for a trip south and stopped by the storage unit after work to grab gear for the road trip. I accidentally stayed after the gated hours allowed and triggered the alarm as I drove out through the gate. A shrill siren blared as I sped down the block to the Metolius offices. I parked quickly, and clicked off all of the interior lights, ducking below the window level in the back of my wagon just as the storage unit manager pulled up. I had to piss so badly but did not dare get out while she patrolled the neighborhood looking for me. She finally gave up the search thirty minutes later, and I breathed a sigh of relief and got ready for another night at Camp Metolius.

The employees at Metolius had diverse backgrounds, but each willingly accepted the sacrifice of lower wages in exchange for the freedoms the relaxed atmosphere and hours afforded them. We all shared a small kitchen area on the second floor, but I dared not leave any food in there as everyone tended to snack indiscriminately on anything left behind. My sister, Miranda, surprised me at the office on my twenty-seventh birthday, hand delivering a dozen of my favorite banana cupcakes. One of my very earliest childhood memories is of my grandmother making these cupcakes every time we visited. Composed of the simple ingredients of overripe bananas and flour, topped with a buttery sweet frosting, they were irresistible. My sister discovered the recipe years after my grandmother passed, and she had absolutely perfected it. I knew if I left the box on the production floor of Metolius, they would be consumed within moments, and I selfishly wanted to keep the treats all to myself. I ate one quickly and then sneaked the remaining eleven cupcakes into the car before heading upstairs to prep the climbing harness webbing pieces for their next step on the sewing room floor.

It's my birthday, why am I working? I thought, and hurried through my tasks, racing to get to the crag and take advantage of the crisp temperatures and low humidity that would make the volcanic rock at Smith sticky for my chalked fingertips and snug-fitting climbing shoes. Movement up a sheer rock face is part faith, part fluid movement, and pure will. Smith Rock is notorious for its cryptic and technical face climbing, requiring impeccable footwork on the dime-sized bumps in the rock face and handholds sometimes barely the thickness of a credit card. I visualized the tiny fingertip handholds on my unclimbed "project"—a rock climbing route slightly above my ability that I was "working," which means I was climbing it repeatedly until my movements became a fluid dance and I could climb it from the ground to the top without falling, using only my hands and feet for upward progress.

Finally, I was free to go, and Denali danced around me, excited for a trip to Smith. He hopped into the back of the Subaru just as I remembered I had forgotten to tell the lead sewer where I'd left the box of harness parts ready for assembly. I dashed back upstairs to the sewing floor and was back within a few minutes. As I drove away, I glanced in the rearview mirror to check in with Denali, and he looked away quickly as I caught his eye. His ears were cocked at an odd angle, and he continued to avoid meeting my gaze.

Noticing a glint of aluminum foil in the mirror, I realized his expression was one of guilt. *Oh no, the cupcakes!* I thought. Pulling off to the roadside, I opened the rear hatch and saw that Denali had indeed consumed the remaining eleven cupcakes in their entirety. I felt frustration flare up and then just laughed. "You sure have great taste, Denali," I said. "I hope you enjoyed those. How's that tummy feeling?" He drank a full bowl of water that evening, but somehow managed to hold all of the cupcakes down without getting sick.

A few months later, I had to fly out for a weeklong trip with my family to Isla Mujeres, so I left Denali under the care of my manager on the Metolius sewing room floor, handing off his food bin, which held a month's supply of kibble. After I returned from my travels, I was in her office chatting and thanking her for watching Denali. I asked her where Denali was, not recognizing the chunky canine at my side.

"He's right beside you!" she exclaimed, laughing.

I glanced down and saw a barrel-shaped dog where one with a slender waistline and defined muscular rear legs should be. He was ecstatic to see me and had been trying to get my attention, but I had ignored the obese dog at my side that barely resembled Denali.

I managed to stammer, "What happened?!" as my manager's son walked in and declared, "Denali always looked hungry and was begging for food, so I felt bad and fed him until he stopped begging." I picked up Denali's food bin, and realized it was empty.

Now I understood the cause of the issue. Denali had eaten a month's worth of food in one week. Kneeling to greet my portly companion, I looked in his eyes and had to laugh at his industriousness. He always knew how to get what he wanted, and this time, it was far too much of a good thing.

"You're going to boot camp," I joked, half-serious. Over the following weeks we ignored the "fat dog" jokes at the crag, and I began increasing his hiking mileage and trail runs once I thought his joints could handle the extra fifteen pounds he carried on his normally sixty-pound frame. He was always excited to be outside, so he rarely lagged behind during our outings. It took a full two months, but Denali's athletic build became more recognizable as he returned to a healthier weight.

Denali had few canine playmates, preferring the company of humans he loved. It wasn't that he disliked other dogs, as he got along with most, I think he just saw that any love he offered to a person would result in head rubs and delicious human treats. Who could blame him, really? His soft eyes could convince anyone with a pulse to offer up the tastiest morsels.

Denali's extroverted nature also led to many of my closest friendships. His northern-breed genetics gave him a tendency to wander, and since he was ruled by his love of both food and human attention, he would often go seeking them while I was distracted in camp.

I would usually stay out at the Grasslands while climbing at my home crag of Smith Rock, and many evenings, Denali would wander off and disappear around dinnertime and be gone for anywhere from five minutes to a couple of hours, often visiting other climbers and exploring the area. There weren't many other climbers there, and the road was a ways away, so I wouldn't get too worried about him, as he always returned.

While climbing at the crag the morning following his escapades, I would often meet someone for the first time, and before I could introduce myself, they would rave about how much they loved Denali.

"You're Denali's dad! He hung out with us last night."

"Last night he visited our camp, and I gave him some leftovers. Denali is such a good dog. Right, Denali?"

As the new friend bent over to give his ears a few scratches, Denali would give them the "I'll do anything for another slice of steak" face. Then the person would look up at me and say, "Oh, by the way, what's your name?"

One serendipitous introduction happened shortly after we arrived at the cobbled walls of Maple Canyon during a climbing trip through Utah. Denali sauntered off during breakfast, following his nose to the bacon and eggs being cooked at the camp next door. I went looking for him and soon was in conversation with Jeremy and Lisa Hensel, a couple who were living out of a truck camper at rock climbing destinations throughout the west. They welcomed Denali into their camp as he played with their two dogs, Maya and Kenai.

As they packed up to leave camp, we chatted for a bit and traded beta—climber speak for detailed information on how to climb a sequence of moves on a route—on their favorite climbing routes in the canyon. A month or so afterward, we were all reunited at Smith Rock, climbing and camping together and sharing stories over dinner in the camper. I felt comfortable opening up about the details of my struggles with the divorce, and Jeremy and Lisa became close friends and confidants. Denali introduced me to many people over the years, and meeting these two was exactly what I needed at the time.

That fall, as the weather grew colder, we all caravanned south to the red desert crack climbs of Indian Creek in Utah, the California granite wonderlands of Bishop and Joshua Tree National Park, and the Red Rock Canyon of Nevada just west of the Las Vegas strip. Jeremy and Lisa were both not only gifted climbers but also very photogenic, and they didn't seem to mind my tagging along to photograph their ascents. Lisa was a photographer as well, so we would take turns shooting photos between climbs.

I was just getting to know the photo editor and marketing director at Metolius, a humble but legendary Yosemite and Smith Rock climber named Brooke Sandahl. I gathered the courage to share a few of my images with Brooke, and to my surprise, he took an interest in my work. My images were the early attempts of an enthusiast, but he was encouraging and offered advice on how I could improve my compositions and angles while shooting climbers in action.

While hanging around Brooke's office, I watched him select images from sheets of slide film on his light table. I began to understand how photos were edited and used for marketing and the annual catalogs.

Brooke received submissions from photographers across the globe, and he showed me the cover letters and photography submissions of the climbing photographer greats of the day, such as Greg Epperson and Jim Thornburg. After my travels that fall with Jeremy and Lisa, I pulled together my favorite shots from the trip, and to my surprise Brooke selected one of them for publication in a Japanese distributor's edition of their catalog. It was a photo of Lisa as she admired the striking prow of a bouldering route called the Mandala in the Buttermilks, glowing in the evening light. Denali had a casual way of slipping into my photographs, and he made a cameo in my first published image by walking through the frame as I depressed the shutter, his muscular rear end and upright tail frozen in time. His confidence in his handsomeness always elevated my photographs, so I never complained.

Seeing my work in print made me dream of one day focusing on photography as a career, but it seemed so unattainable. I was fascinated by the photographs found on the pages of the Patagonia catalogs, the photographic holy grail of outdoor lifestyle, featuring most of the top adventure photographers in the industry. The images spoke of the lifestyle I had been questing for since I took the job at Earth's Edge. The owner of the gear shop, Karl Tucker, was a mountain climber, and he helped introduce my small-town Michigan kid mind to an unfamiliar world where individuals dedicated themselves to a life that prioritized time outdoors, honing their crafts in the mountains, climbing crags, rivers, and oceans. My perspective would never be the same after that. I had been raised off the grid under challenging circumstances, so it was not the discomfort I craved, it was pursuing one's passions on nature's canvas, finding community within the like-minded wanderers who followed the same rhythms of tide and stone and weather in pursuit of their adventures.

In my free time away from the Metolius office, I continued to document my climbing trips during the fall and winter circuit, splitting my time among Indian Creek, Bishop and Joshua Tree National Park, and Red Rock Canyon. I set aside my favorite images along the way, until I had forty total, just enough to fill up two slide sheets. I wrote a cover letter and addressed it to the Patagonia photo department and tried to ignore the voice of doubt that my photography was not good enough.

Weeks later, a response arrived from Jane Sievert, the lead photo editor at Patagonia. I sat with Denali in my van in the afternoon sunshine and held my breath as I tore open the letter. Jane wrote that she was holding four images in Patagonia's archives and planned to publish two of them in that summer's European catalog.

Friends had been suggesting that perhaps my growing passion for photography could be turned into a career, but I'd always brushed them off. But when my copies arrived and I saw my images featured in a Patagonia catalog, I felt a spark of possibility. Denali looked at me, his eyes dancing in excitement, his tail thumping the bench seat as I stared at my images printed in the catalog. He had known all along, but now I felt it too. If Jane and Brooke both saw something in my work, then maybe this was a career worth pursuing and could become the key to living a life outdoors, where Denali and I could roam free.

Because of the shy child that still lives within me, it often took me several days to finally summon the courage to call Jane at her office. I would dial up her office number on my Motorola flip phone, hang up before it rang, and then pace the Smith Rock parking lot and try again. These days I have learned to overcome this fear, and when I am at my healthiest, I can achieve a flow state when networking at events and make deep connections.

After ten months living out of the back of my Subaru, I was getting

weary of the cramped space and the constant gear shuffle every morning and night to make room for sleep, and began to daydream about
other options. After a long day of climbing at Smith Rock, I was exhausted and decided to sleep at the edge of the Walmart parking lot
in Redmond in the back of my Subaru instead of driving back to Bend.

Unaware that a train track ran parallel to the parking lot, I drifted
off to sleep only to be jolted awake by a drawn-out blast of a locomo-
tive's horn. This was the first of what seemed like twenty trains, so I
slept fitfully but stuck it out until morning.

The following morning, I was blearily attempting to lay out the day's
work on the cutting room table when my co-worker Ron came in and
handed me a slip of paper with a woman's name and a phone number.

"Are you setting me up on a date?" I asked. "No," he laughed. "Just
call that number right now. There's the perfect camper van for sale,
and it's insanely cheap. I would buy it but my girlfriend won't let me.
Dude. It's an epic deal . . . just call the number!" I obliged, and that
afternoon I upgraded to a new tiny home on wheels.

It was a 1987 Ford E-250 Get-Away Van, a fully converted camper
with just over sixty thousand miles on the odometer. I sold my Subaru
to the mayor's son, a skier who was stoked about the bed in the back,
which I'd assembled on that same cutting room table where I was
working when I found out about the van that would be my new home
for the next three years.

That same week, a retired man at the grocery store asked if he could
take a peek inside my van, my first taste of the enthusiastic van life
community that seems to span all ages and demographics.

"Really nice," he said as he admired the setup. "It's similar to my
1988 model. You mind if I ask how much you paid for it? I got mine
for $12,000."

"I paid $2,750," I said. His shocked expression made me realize that I had lucked into the perfect camping rig, and even though my Metolius paychecks were slim, I was debt-free and living my dream life.

The van was spare yet adequate. It had an eighty-watt solar panel and two six-volt golf cart batteries, which powered my laptop, slide scanner, and printer through a four-hundred-watt inverter I bought for thirty dollars. That invertor lasted for five years, even after I disconnected the cooling fan to quiet it down. My refrigerator did not work when I first bought the van, so I removed it and utilized that space with three large drawers that served as bins for my food. I thoroughly tested my theory that eggs do not need refrigeration, and never once got sick on the two dozen eggs a week that served as my main protein source during those years in the van.

I had a three-burner propane stove and a furnace that came in handy during the long cold nights of winter, especially at the higher elevation and desert areas that would freeze in the night. My friends would go to bed by six on some nights, but I simply couldn't sleep longer than eight or nine hours, so I would snuggle up with Denali and read late into the evening or watch movies I had rented. There was more time to relax then with none of the smartphone distractions of today.

Van life was typically a peaceful affair as my camper resembled more of a miniature retiree motor home than a dirtbag climber rig. However, on the eve of my very first photo shoot gig for Metolius, I decided to camp in the parking lot of the climbing gym in order to not risk being late for what seemed to me then a once-in-a-lifetime opportunity. A paid photo shoot! How did I get so lucky?

I was getting ready for bed, and had the lights dimmed in the van. I had just thrown on my Patagonia silkweight boxers, the only clothing I can tolerate while sleeping, and was just getting settled in with my book, a reread of *Lord of the Rings*. I blasted the furnace to take off the evening chill, and Denali curled up under my arm to share some body heat. The small space of my van heated quickly and had just started getting a little warm when Denali jumped off the bed to get a drink of water.

Immediately after his feet hit the floor, I heard a fierce pounding on the side doors. Spotlights streamed through the cracks in my curtains, seemingly from every direction.

A megaphone blared, "Bend Police—please exit the vehicle!"

Flabbergasted, I felt my heart race as I tried to figure out what I possibly had done that was illegal. I got dressed as quickly as I could, but my delay in opening the doors only seemed to piss off the cops outside, and the beating on the doors became more insistent.

"Come out *now*. With your hands up!"

"I'm coming, sheesh," I whispered as Denali growled at the intruders outside. As soon as I clicked open the lock, the doors were ripped open and I was yanked by my wrists, almost going fully horizontal in my exit. Denali growled in protest as I was hurled outside.

"Is there anyone else inside?" the officer yelled.

"Just my dog and me, ma'am."

She jumped inside the van to search it after turning me over to one of the other four officers that surrounded the van. A fifth stepped from the shadows as my feet were kicked apart and I was aggressively patted down. I realized there were at least three patrol cars.

"Can I ask what I've done wrong?"

"We had a report called in by a citizen in this neighborhood of a suspicious vehicle with a struggle going on inside."

I chuckled at the neighbor that must've seen my van parked and wanted that sketchy character out of there as soon as possible. It was my first night there, so they must have been extra paranoid.

The first officer emerged from my van and gave the all clear. "It's actually really cozy in there," she said.

"Yeah, glad I cleaned up today," I quipped drily.

"You're free to go," she said.

"Uh, thanks?" I murmured as I thought about how both the neighbor and the police had profiled me as either a troublemaker or a homeless person, even though my little home suited my needs perfectly.

If I remember correctly, the shoot paid only around $150, plus film and processing, but the experience seemed worth it at the time. A lot of my images were soft or blurry because my old Nikon N90s didn't focus all that well in the studio lights. Now with digital and especially my newer Sony mirrorless cameras, it's easy to catch those errors, but back then you could not look at the back of your camera to see if you had nailed a shot.

Yet the excitement of ripping open a package from the lab and looking at the slides on a light table for the first time is hard to grasp in today's smartphone era of instant gratification.

Seeing the potential in my photography, Brooke suggested I attend the Outdoor Retailer show to see if I could find more brands to work with. The massive trade show that used to be held in Salt Lake City, and now takes place in Denver, is an event at which every brand remotely affiliated with the outdoor industry has a presence. I was overwhelmed by the spectacle of it all, but saw opportunity for making a career out of something I enjoyed immensely: taking pictures. I returned to Bend and felt myself at a crossroads. Denali and I hiked to the summit of Tumalo Mountain, a hike near Mount Bachelor. I found a vista and sat overlooking the peaks nearby. I spoke my thoughts aloud, asking Denali what my next steps should be.

"Hey, D, should I quit Metolius? Would I ever be able to make enough through photography to feed us? Metolius did offer money toward job training, but would it make sense to go to photography school? Brooks Institute of Photography costs like $100K. There's no way I could swing that!"

I looked down and saw a hawk feather lying nearby. Picking it up, I looked at Denali and asked, "Hey, bud, are you ready to fly? Let's do this!" He leaned closer, reassuring me that I had his support no matter what lay in store for us.

> Let's go! I just want to spend every day romping out in
> nature with you. Can we stock the van with lots of treats?

Denali wagged his tail, looked up at me, and then sprinted down the trail, leading the way to an unknown future.

I stopped by Metolius to put in a few hours, and my manager called me into her office. "I see you have really taken an interest in photography, that's really great. We need to lay a few people off and I wondered if you'd be willing to be one of them?" Stunned by the serendipitous timing of her question, I paused for a moment. I had been at Metolius for eighteen months, and there was not really a future in working there. I was feeling drawn to photography and the adventures that lay ahead, but the uncertainty was terrifying. This was the nudge I needed, a gentle yet obvious push toward a new life.

"Yes," I answered. "I think it's time I see what this whole photography thing is all about." I hugged her and thanked her for my time there and said my goodbyes. Denali sensed the change and paced the storage unit parking lot restlessly as I packed up the van. The plan was to head north to Squamish, British Columbia, and I had no idea what would follow after that. All I knew is the open road beckoned, and we were heeding the call.

Every summer, West Coast rock climbers would make a pilgrimage up Interstate 5 through Seattle and up to Bellingham, entering Canadian soil through the Peace Arch, until the urban reaches of Vancouver, British Columbia, gave way to the scenic Sea to Sky Highway snaking its way north to the recreational towns of Squamish, Whistler, and Pemberton. The first, Squamish, is a climbers' paradise with the sheer granite walls of the Stawamus Chief towering 702 meters (2,303 feet) over the waters of the Howe Sound, with boulders perfectly shaped for climbing littering the forested floor at the base of the wall.

Surrounded on three sides by salt water, a thin man-made peninsula called the Spit thrusts out beyond a gorgeous estuary and into the sound with spectacular views of the Chief. In the years before kiteboarding became popular and made the Spit a popular launching point, it was the ideal place to park the van in solitude after a long day of climbing, and to camp with Denali.

Each morning, I would throw open the side doors to let the sunshine and fresh ocean breeze slowly warm and wake me. Nothing could be heard except the song of seabirds and the bark of sea lions, so I would let Denali roam as I dozed in the morning sunlight. I was jarred out of my peaceful semilucid meditation by Denali jumping onto the bed. Before I could finish saying, "Hey, buddy," I almost puked at the horrific smell emanating from his thin fur coat.

"Off the bed!" I grunted as I choked back the nausea and pulled on a pair of jeans. I sped into town to my friend's place to use her garden hose. While I scrubbed Denali with Dr. Bronner's soap, my friend laughed and said, "It's that season. The fall Chinook run was thick this year—my dogs think rolling in salmon carcasses is a sport." Denali looked insulted but tolerated my attempts to mask the aroma of rotting fish with the lathered peppermint soap. After this happened for the second consecutive morning, I stopped opening the doors until I was awake enough to keep an eye on him. Fortunately, he never contracted the horrible parasite found in salmon carcasses that I now am aware kills many dogs in the Pacific Northwest each year.

————

DENALI AND I FOUND OUR GROOVE IN THE HUMBLE LIFESTYLE OF A LOOSE-knit tribe of adventure seekers that traveled between climbing crags and surf breaks throughout the American West. *Dirtbag* is a term prized by those who put time outdoors ahead of the mainstream creature comforts and perceived security of consistent salaries and home mortgages. In many ways, it was easy living, thanks to its simplicity, but it was full of its own challenges. Searching for a quiet place to park Big Blue, my camper van and home on wheels, was a daily challenge. Without a steady paycheck and earning only the meager royalties from my early days of freelancing, I struggled to make ends meet to pay for the fuel for my van, film and developing costs, and food for Denali and me.

Yet the benefits of waking up far from the din of civilization in a place of my choosing and allowing the cycles of the sun and weather to dictate the activities of the day had their own allure. The shorter days of autumn triggered a journey south to Red Rock Canyon; the Virgin River Gorge, a limestone climbing area just over the freeway in the northwest corner of Arizona; El Potrero Chico; Joshua Tree

National Park; and Bishop. Campfires were sparked earlier, and the sleeping hours stretched deep into the warmer midmorning hours. These were blissful years prior to LTE signals reaching into the most remote locales and before the continuous allure of distraction was delivered via today's tiny supercomputers in our pockets. Checking email happened at local libraries, which offered a supply of books for the long evenings that started as early as four p.m. around the solstice.

Big Blue was equipped with a furnace, so while my campmates would dive into their warm sleeping bags and tents immediately following dinner, I would read book after book with the heat blasting, fighting to stay awake until at least nine p.m. Some evenings, I would squeeze six or more fellow climbers into my van for dinner parties while Denali patrolled the floor for dropped scraps and hands offering a head scratch or a morsel under the table.

Denali and I would also host movie nights, and I would plug my laptop into a modest seventeen-inch Apple Cinema Display, a nearly square screen surrounded by a gaudy clear plastic shroud. The sound played through my stereo system, and we would all pack into the bed like sardines, with Denali nestled in, absolutely in heaven within the cuddle pile. For intermission, everyone would hop out to stare at the stars while we relieved ourselves, then dive back into the warmth for the final act. If my battery was getting low, we would all rotate to whoever's camper had power to spare, or say good night.

Springtime started the northward migration. Bishop stayed in season until April, as did the splitter cracks and mellow sandstone vibes of Indian Creek. Smith Rock was good until late June, as long as you chased the shade. Midsummer was far too hot and miserable to climb the technical faces, and oppressive heat would beckon the crew across the border to Canada, finding reprieve among the granite boulders and walls of Squamish, British Columbia, or the picturesque crags of the Canadian Rockies around Banff and Canmore.

My daily routine was simple, yet rarely dull. Rigging ropes on sheer rock faces to photograph a rock climb in the glow of the evening light, sharing stories around a flickering campfire into the early morning hours, selecting and scanning my best slides and mailing them to the photo editors at Patagonia and *Climbing* and *Rock and Ice* magazines, exploring untouched desert canyons with Denali for potential climbing lines, tending to fingers and forearms aching from the physical abuse of rock climbing—these, to me, were the elements of a life well lived. Sharing it with a dog who appreciated time outdoors made it all the richer.

After I was laid off from Metolius, I tried my hand as a sled dog handler in Bend working with over a hundred dogs at a kennel to the east of town, with Jerry Scdoris and his daughter Rachael, the first legally blind racer to complete the Iditarod race in Alaska. I guided a few corporate team-building retreats around Mount Bachelor, guiding tours in nighttime blizzards. During a stormier afternoon on the mountain, I clipped Denali into the staked-out line with the other sled dogs. Ten minutes later, I found him in a ball shivering miserably. He looked up at me with such pitiful eyes that I couldn't leave him there any longer. "Half-husky but definitely not a big fan of the cold, eh, D?" His pit bull genetics left him without much insulation on his underside, so he often crawled on top of my pack during crisp days at Smith Rock while I climbed, and I'd often wrap him in my puffy jackets so he could lie down and sleep. This time, my only option was to place him gently into one of the small bunks on the sled dog truck. I opened the small twenty-inch-square door at face level and hoisted him into the straw-lined kennel. Denali wriggled in protest but quickly accepted the shelter from the chill that the confined space allowed.

Denali was rarely on a leash, a prohibited act in a national park, and his wanderings could be worrisome considering coyotes that frequented the area. Rumor had it, sometimes the coyotes would use a lone scout to lure dogs away from camp to play, then attack the unwitting pup as a group. Denali dodged both coyotes and park rangers and seemed to have an uncanny knack for disappearing every time the rangers patrolled the climber campground. I had heard of friends' dogs who hid on the command "Ranger!" but Denali seemed to just know things without being told.

In the years that followed, Denali's athleticism would become apparent. He had broad muscular shoulders that tapered to a tiny waist, followed by bulging quadriceps. My friends often teased me, saying, "Owners always look like their dogs—look at you and D! Wide shoulders and tiny waist . . . like Mr. Incredible."

With climbing as my main focus outside of photography, Denali and I shared countless days in the canyons and gullies of Smith Rock, exploring every angle, putting up new routes, and working on the harder climbs or "projects" that I hoped to complete. There were a few areas in the park that were easy fifth class or exposed fourth class— meaning a fall could cause serious injury or death. I would carefully lift Denali through these sections as we ascended and keep a tight hold on his leash or harness as we navigated the trickier approaches.

Denali began to develop enough confidence that it became safer for him to descend off leash on his own instead of with my help. He had the bouldery descent down to the basalt climbs at Northern Point wired, and when the loose and treacherous tunnel—formed by massive fifty-foot boulders stacked atop one another—up into Cocaine Gully was still open, he would deftly descend each tier to safety. This trail is now permanently closed after a boulder fell from high above and lodged into the old tunnel. Other approaches into the gullies required me to carry him over my shoulder through narrow chimneys that I would shinny up. In those moments, Denali had an unquestioning trust, and would never struggle, as he understood this would send both of us tumbling to the rocks below.

At Smith Rock, Denali was off leash whenever it was safer for him or when I knew we were in an area the rangers never patrolled. To get to the "backside," we would climb over Asterisk Pass, a notch with a few exposed climbing moves about fifty feet off the ground. From there, it is a narrow ramp less than two feet wide that slopes to the ground. Usually, I would carefully navigate this descent while carrying Denali in one arm, sinking my other hand into a crack "hand jam," which I used as a safety anchor to keep us steady as I moved my feet down the wall. Once we were at the ramp, I would set Denali down and "belay" him on his leash while I trotted down the narrow ramp. When it was safe to do so, I would let go of his leash and he'd finish the last twenty feet on his own, as there was nothing for his leash to catch on.

Denali's proudest moment was when he learned to descend this fully unassisted, an unplanned event he decided to do on his own. Denali was running up ahead as we hiked up to the large "Asterisk Boulder" precariously perched atop the pass. I saw there was a large group of helmeted climbers being guided in over the pass, using ropes to rappel one by one to the other side. Before I could even call out Denali's name, he saw his descent route was clear. As a new climber listened to instructions from the guide on how to descend, Denali shot forward, sliding among all the waiting students, nimbly navigating the move I had always carefully carried him down, somehow contorting his body to turn the corner in time to avoid tumbling over the sheer face. He sprinted down the ramp, stopping and turning at the bottom to wait for me. I was nearly as stunned as the guide and the group that he had just lectured on the dangers of this place. Denali had been carried through it many times before and had made up his mind that he was fully capable of doing it on his own. I have seen some dogs leap without looking, but Denali was always cautious, calculated, yet confident when the moment left little room for error. As he waited for me at the bottom of the descent, he pranced proudly back and forth, a huge grin wrinkling his wide jawline.

The only time I was ever truly frightened for his safety was when we crossed the Crooked River to the Upper Gorge during a time when the river-polished basalt boulders were exposed by a lower flow. Leading the way, he leaped from rock to rock before slipping on a small boulder that was polished almost as smooth as glass. His hindquarters were underwater, getting sucked toward a deep "hole" in the current of the turbulent river. He held on with his front legs, staring at me with eyes that calmly relayed an SOS. He was in trouble and knew it. Behind him I could see the deep keeper hole—a recirculating current on the upstream side of a boulder that can pin you underwater indefinitely—and I immediately got into position to grab his collar. I always kept his collars loose so he could slip them if they got caught on a branch or fence, and now the collar began to slide. Denali's eyes widened, and my heart raced as he felt the current pulling him away from me. I reset my hand firmly on the scruff of his neck, braced my feet against the boulders on either side, and fought steadily against the suction of the river. He pushed as I pulled, and finally, I felt the keeper current release him. He shook off and panted heavily, well aware of the danger we had narrowly avoided. A month later I heard a student drowned in that same area, and his body did not reappear for quite some time.

In the city, Denali usually seemed bored and listless, lacking the stimulation and variance of nature. On the road, there were times while traveling where Denali would enter an altered state, almost seeming like his feral side overtook him until he got his bearings. It was almost always at stops along the way, never at our final destination. I learned that this lasted only five or ten minutes, so I would keep him on a leash until he had his bearings and felt safe in his new environment.

While driving north from Bishop up US 395 highway through the Eastern Sierra, I made a pee stop north of Mammoth Lakes. I was standing next to the van wearing Chaco flip-flops, and Denali tweaked out and ran a half mile up a tree-lined mountainside in knee-deep snow. I tracked him and found him standing near the summit waiting for me, tongue hanging out as he seemed to laugh at my predicament. My feet were numb and freezing, but I was so relieved to find Denali that I didn't feel a thing. I came back to my van on the side of the highway to see the side doors to my home that contained nearly all of my possessions (which, fortunately, were all still there) wide open, just how I'd left them.

THE FIRST FEW YEARS OF MY PHOTOGRAPHY CAREER, I WAS MAKING BE-tween $5K and $10K a year. My overhead was low, only gasoline, food, and gear, and no rent. Rock climbing burned a lot of calories, so in order to stay fueled for my adventures, I scoured grocery liquidators for boxes of old energy bars and ramen and foraged for recently expired yet unspoiled cuisine in the dumpsters of Whole Foods and Trader Joe's. During my childhood, my family prioritized our scant resources toward simple bodily sustenance and secondhand clothing rather than ski passes or other luxuries, and this stripped-down existence on the road while I barely scraped by during the early years of my career bore many similarities to my younger years.

My dad worked the night shift at a steel foundry, and during his waking daylight hours he taught himself how to build a home and constructed a functional off-the-grid house. It would not pass many of the building codes of today, but it kept us sheltered from the harsh Michigan winters. We pumped our well water, heated our home with a woodstove, read by the light of kerosene lanterns, and warmed up bathwater in a teakettle on a propane stove. Our toilet was a small camping porta-potty for emergencies when it was too cold, but we mostly used the outhouse out back. A childhood daydream was to immerse myself fully in an overflowing tub of steaming bathwater.

From the perspective of today's screen-addicted society, this was a unique upbringing. I was often teased for not having a television and for being clueless when my classmates laughed about the latest episode of a show. Instead, the woods offered me endless entertainment as I searched for treasures and made up games.

I learned to help slaughter chickens for their meat, plucking the feathers and gathering the eggs from the free-roaming hens we kept for that purpose. My dad hunted deer out of necessity, not for sport, and at times when our stock of food ran low, he bent the rules of the hunting seasons to keep us fed. We all pitched in to care for the large garden, tending to the vegetables. We had a tiny propane-powered refrigerator, so during the harvest season my mom would spend countless hours in a steam-filled kitchen, pressure canning or pickling the meat and vegetables to store in the root cellar my dad had installed beneath the house. From the distance of memory, the off-grid simple living has a romantic feel, but it was a challenging upbringing. The stress of never quite having enough to feed a family of four took its toll on my parents. I have memories of receiving government food aid before I was old enough to feel embarrassed by it.

My parents never criticized my van-dwelling lifestyle. Mom would ask, "Where you at?" each time I called, a habit I found equally endearing and annoying. "We were camping in hotel parking lots when you were a baby," she'd say, recalling stories of their wanders around the southern US and into Mexico. I appreciated their support as I traded the tree branches of my youth for sheer rock faces, my beloved pencils and sketch paper for a camera and film, yard sales that clothed me through my childhood for Patagonia's outlet stores and sample bins, the welfare cheese for expired food from grocery store dumpsters. It was not romantic; it was simply survival. It was a means to an end. Somewhere on the horizon was relief from the heartbreak and depression and scrounging to keep myself fed. I saw that pursuing climbing would never satiate the void I felt, and hoped that photography would bring me there, wherever there was.

After a day of climbing in Red Rock Canyon, I was knee-deep in a Trader Joe's dumpster in Las Vegas, picking through the unopened bricks of cheese, the shrink-wrapped vegetables, and pizza dough, all of which had "expired" that day. Back then, Trader Joe's was a gold mine for climbers on the road, and we made dozens of pizzas made only with ingredients scavenged from the dumpster.

It was nearly dark and I was completely focused on gathering as much of this bountiful smorgasbord as I could, when I was startled by the sight of a man standing between me and my van. My feet shifted among the discarded food items; something about the man's demeanor and movements instinctually sent me into high alert. "You okay, man? You need help?"

I was wearing a classy Patagonia wool sweater I had scored for twelve dollars at the outlet store, and had to laugh at the irony of the situation. What was this seemingly well-dressed, twentysomething guy with a camper van doing standing in this back-alley dumpster?

"Yeah, man, I'm all good," I muttered, staring past my new acquaintance at Big Blue's driver's side door, which I had left wide open with the keys still in the ignition. Denali was in there, along with my camera gear and laptop and every material possession that I needed for living. I subconsciously reached out to Denali and said, "Hey, boy, you gotta handle this if he tries to get the van." Denali stared through the curtains of the van window as I analyzed how to maneuver out of this situation.

> Don't worry about a thing. I've got your back. You just find
> me some treats in that dumpster and we're all good.

Looking me up and down, he thought I might still have something to offer and proceeded on into a lengthy and well-rehearsed story of why he desperately needed the cash for a ride to see his sick girlfriend, who was all alone and suffering in the hospital.

I kept eye contact as I carried a box stacked full of my food for the week, fancy cheeses and fresh artichoke hearts and dented coffee tins, walking straight past him until I could reach my van door. I pretended to look for cash in the door pocket as I reached into the console and wrapped my hand around my keys. I looked back at Denali and breathed a sigh of relief. He looked concerned, but I did not have time to reassure him. Turning back to the man, I said, "So sorry, all I have is this loose change." Handing it over, I quickly hopped in the van and drove away. Denali kept an attentive eye on our surroundings, growling fiercely if anyone approached the van. Having him with me, I rarely felt unsafe, but the incident shook me, and I swore I would be more careful, especially in cities. Referring to the easy and worry-free living around Indian Creek and Moab, I joked to Denali, "We aren't in the desert anymore," as I shared some of the evening's dumpster cuisine with him.

Denali was indiscriminate when it came to the food he consumed but was meticulous about how he received affection. As I stroked his head, Denali would subtly lift his chin, guiding my fingers to exactly the spot of his choosing, eventually leading me to scratch every part of his ears, neck, head, and chin.

He would often attempt to return the favor, and after long days of climbing, he would try to lick my sweaty, salt-crusted arms. I would usually push him away, but after a particularly hot May day of desert crack climbing in Indian Creek, I obliged. In silent fascination, I sat watching as he methodically groomed every surface of my arms without missing a single spot of salt. I wondered if this was more of a dirtbag or a dog lover moment, my allowing Denali to give me a "shower" without any complaint.

During my time sleeping in my car or over the van life years, I had always taken a level of pride in never looking or smelling like a dirtbag. I found that a sink shower and clean hair went a long way toward a relatively accepting public while out in the real world. Although others were okay with five years of aluminum—from climbing carabiners—and climbing chalk, body oils, desert dirt, and food permanently staining their puffy insulated jackets, I tried to visit the laundromat on a semiregular basis. Same with Denali, unless he needed a mandatory post-skunk-encounter shower. I made sure to at least play fetch with him in the river or mountain lakes to keep his fur fluffy and soft. For both of us, maintaining a level of hygiene kept our lives richer with the company of friends and potential love interests who wanted to stroke his fur, or my hair. Denali and I were dirtbags, yes, but no one else was the wiser.

4

First Blood

Joshua Tree National Park, which straddles the Colorado and Mojave Deserts in Southern California, is a granite playground frequented by climbers during the long winters that bring unfavorable climbing conditions to most of the crags farther north. Its miles of sun-kissed domes and infinite stretches of Joshua trees, a cartoonlike plant with an unmistakable spiky silhouette, make for a climber's paradise.

One evening in December 2002, I was sitting around the campfire at Hidden Valley Campground in the park. Denali and I were joined by Haven and Bo, two climbing partners I was sharing the campsite with. I stood up to stoke the fire, and the glowing embers blurred to amorphous blobs across my visual field as my knees buckled and I collapsed onto the coarse granitic soil. I awoke in a heap and felt Denali nuzzling me as he frantically licked my cheeks in concern. As I slowly became aware of my surroundings, I saw a look of deep worry on Bo's face and realized I had fainted.

Brushing off my fall as a minor dizzy spell, I muttered an excuse that I needed more iron in my diet. I had been living full time out of my van for eight months, and Big Blue didn't have a refrigerator, so storing meat was not an option. Besides, my meager early photography income allowed little room to budget for anything except the calorie-dense meals my body craved, fueling long days of rock climbing with Denali and my climbing partners. Accessing many of the areas required long approaches to the climbing routes, and my pack was usually stuffed with climbing hardware, ropes, camera gear, and extra water for Denali.

By the next morning, my concern about my collapse had faded, and after breakfast I took care of business in a park service pit toilet as Haven and Bo racked up for the day's climbing objectives. Within the pungent and cell-like concrete facilities, I tried to hurry, both to avoid the awful smell and to not keep my friends waiting. I wiped and stopped cold, gasping in a full breath of the foul air as I stared down, a bright red strip of blood ominously imprinted on the toilet paper.

Startled, my mind reeled as I grabbed my pack from camp, trying to act normal. I could tell that Denali knew something was amiss. He always knew. I knelt down and scratched his ears. "It's okay, D, I'm sure it's nothing serious."

> You look worried . . . should I be worried? When you fell down in camp, I had to lick you to wake you up! Something is wrong . . . you get tired so easily and don't want to romp with me for as long as you used to. Something's up, man.

I stifled my intuition that there was something very wrong until a month later when I confided what had happened to a friend while climbing in Red Rock Canyon. After I explained my symptoms, she stared at me for a moment before replying.

"You could have colon cancer."

She shared these words without emotion, as if stating an immutable fact. Shocked, my mind began to spin, seeking any other explanation. That night, I researched the symptoms in hopes of disproving her theory. I found an online questionnaire listing the signs of colon cancer and felt a sense of redemption after reading the first line:

"Are you over 50?"

I sighed in relief, which only blinded me to the damning questions that followed:

Do you have blood in your stool?
Any gas or bloating?

My subconscious diverted its senses as I skimmed over the final line:

Seek medical attention if you see blood or any of these symptoms are present.

As my symptoms steadily worsened over the next eighteen months, I was constantly recalibrating what "normal" digestion was to me. If I was bloated and the toilet was stained with blood, I would simply come up with new excuses to justify why it had occurred, reasoning with myself that I must have a food allergy. If I hit a bump and crapped my pants while mountain biking, I would clean up the mess and pull out the fresh pair of underwear that I always carried with me.

I devoured books on diet and digestion, desperately trying to understand on my own what was happening and to avoid going to the doctor. I often confided in my close friend Jenny Uchisa (now Jurek) about my new dietary theories.

Jenny lived in Seattle and worked for Montrail, an early manufacturer of trail-running shoes. We first met when I called the customer service line to ask if I could order a pair of shoes at a discounted rate because I worked in the outdoor industry. When I said my name, she was starstruck, thinking I was the legendary English climber also named Ben Moon.

This comical issue of mistaken identity has persisted to this day, and I am still often tagged in photos on social media and receive the occasional email meant for the "other" Ben Moon. Back before he started his current rock climbing brand called Moon Climbing, he would send me posters for his now-defunct clothing brand S7, signing them "I wish I had a name as cool as you."

Jenny and I became close friends after meeting in person at the Outdoor Retailer show, and I would visit her often in Seattle and go see bands play when they toured through town. One evening after watching Matt Costa play at a small venue, we were in line ordering a vegan pizza, and Jenny looked at me with concern as I doubled over in pain. "My stomach hurts so bad and I'm super gassy. I think I'm allergic to bananas and dairy," I fumbled. "Well, I'm allergic to garlic," she said, trying to make me feel better.

Later that weekend, during a hard-fought game of Ping-Pong in her basement, I showed her a book about eating right for my blood type and pronounced, "My blood type is A-positive, so I must just be averse to nightshades. No more eggplants or tomatoes." As if the books on eating properly for my blood type or far-out theories of various food allergies could possibly hold the answers. I was simply desperate to understand my erratic bowels and the monster terrorizing me from within.

The other day, I called Jenny to catch up, and she reminisced about the time I was sick.

Every time you would come up to visit, you'd be like, "Ugh my stomach is upset."

There would always be something, but I never really thought it was anything but a food allergy, because every correlation to your pain you would find something in your diet that was causing the issue.

It seemed like you just wanted to figure it out or find out if you were allergic to food or something. You weren't complaining at all. I don't really feel like it was on your radar as a pressing problem.

Because it just seemed like you were thriving otherwise in your life and healthy. I loved your lifestyle and your friends, and everything about how you were living your life . . . even though you had all your stuff in storage and lived in a big blue van. You were just friends with all the cool kids in the climbing scene.

You know when people are sick? You can see it in their face. You just didn't seem sick at all, and you didn't act sick either. Maybe things were easier to overlook because you were younger and weren't living a "comfortable" lifestyle anyway, just living the van life without a house or anything.

I remember thinking, "Whoa, this is crazy. How did you live with this for so long and not know about it?"

I was acutely aware of the abnormal nature of the symptoms I was experiencing, yet they were inconsistent enough that on the days when I was feeling only minor discomfort, it was easier to just blow them off than to face the reality of how sick I really was. One day the toilet bowl would be splattered with blood, and the very next day there wouldn't be a trace. I would be super bloated, then fine, and so it was easier to blame it on food than to do anything else about it. It seemed more annoying than worrisome, but I knew deep down that I should get it checked out. I was in a level of deep denial, ignoring that my stool had narrowed to half its normal diameter and other signs that something was very wrong. In spite of all indications pointing to a major illness, I hoped to discover a more minor cause and just move on with my life.

Jenny was in design school and newly single and came to visit me a year before I was diagnosed. She had always dreamed of climbing two of the popular multi-pitch climbs at Smith Rock, Zebra Zion and the West Face Variation to the Pioneer route on the Monkey Face. To cheer her up after being dumped by an insensitive boyfriend, I offered to climb both of them with her. While we were up on the wall, Denali ate every last bit of Jenny's snacks, looking smug with a side of heartburn. She was a college student on a limited budget, and Denali had eaten every last morsel of her food for the week, which she had meticulously shopped for at the local co-op. She held a joking grudge toward Denali for years after that, glaring at him while smiling and teasing, "You ate my snacks. Do you remember that?"

Yup. They were delicious . . . but sheesh, do vegans ever
feel full? I could've eaten more and not felt full. I was so
gassy later too. Oof.

When I look at photos now from back then, I can see that I was
gaunt and my cheeks were sucked in, but it was so gradual that it was
hard to recognize at the time.

In the winter of 2004, I was shooting photos with Sonnie Trotter
at the Virgin River Gorge. Sonnie is a Canadian professional climber
I had met four years earlier during the challenging winter when Melanie left. He had given me a lot of encouragement to push my climbing
limits, and his words helped me to send my first 5.13.

On this trip to the Virgin River Gorge, I had been attempting to
redpoint—a term climbers use for sending a climb by climbing from
the ground to the top anchors without falling or resting on gear—a
fun and athletic endurance route rated 5.13a called Joe Six Pack, but
I kept running out of energy before I clipped the anchors. To get
loosened up for another go, I hopped onto Mentor, a 5.12b warm-up
that had a no-hands rest halfway up the climb. When I reached the
halfway point in the climb, my friend was giving me a belay and had
a huge loop of slack out while I rested and shook my arms to rid them
of the lactic acid "pump." Without warning, my body went limp, releasing the tension I'd held by pressing my legs against each wall in
the "stemming" position. I shot out into the emptiness and fell twenty-
five feet before the slack tightened and my belayer's safety device finally caught me.

"Whoa! What happened?!" he yelled up at me as he lowered me to
the ground where Denali stood waiting. "Sorry I had so much slack
out, but no one ever falls there!"

Denali licked my face as I began to slowly untie my knot that was now tightened from the fall.

> Something's wrong, bro. You smell kinda funny. And are even more tired. You sleep so much. And fall a lot. I'm worried, please be okay!

"I have no idea," I told Sonnie. "I just fell out of the rest! It was like my body just gave up."

I decided to give my project a try anyway. I worked through the most difficult moves and battled waves of utter exhaustion and nausea as I fought through the long sequences on the pocketed headwall.

What is happening to me? I thought. *Something simply is not right.*

After clipping the anchors at the top, I felt wave after wave of an overpowering fatigue lay over me, like a pile of lead blankets.

At the base of the climb, I dug through my pack and found an extra fleece top, rolled it into a pillow, and invited Denali to curl up next to me. He nudged my arm, then licked my cheek to wake me up two hours later. His comforting warmth helped me maintain a sense of steadiness and normalcy amid my steadily increasing alarm at my condition. I looked up past Denali's concerned gaze and saw Sonnie standing above me. "Wow, bro, you were out cold. I was really starting to worry about you."

This was not normal, but I was just trying to face each day as it came while I searched for some reason why I felt this way.

A few weeks before my diagnosis, my sister handed me a yellow wristband that read "Live Strong," and mentioned that she and a few other cycling teammates were going to begin selling them to raise money for Lance Armstrong's new cancer foundation. It sounded like a great cause, so I put it on my left wrist, unaware of the cancerous cells reproducing rapidly within my abdomen. Once I was diagnosed, that yellow band of rubber encircling my wrist became a source of strength and solidarity, and I did not take it off for two years.

That same week I received an email from the photo editor at *Rock and Ice* and *Trail Runner* magazine. He told me that the magazines would publish my images on the covers of the upcoming issues. I was ecstatic.

Magazine covers, two of them? At the same time?! I feel like a real photographer now.

Denali looked at me, his eyes dancing. I knew exactly what he was thinking.

I told you so!

My photographs would be printed on the cover of the June 2004 editions of both mags. The *Rock and Ice* climbing cover was of Sonnie Trotter on his bold first traditional—all gear, no bolts—free ascent of the east face of Monkey Face at Smith Rock, where I had dangled in space three hundred feet off the valley floor, spinning endlessly on the rope fixed above Sonnie as he climbed, an April storm bombarding us with wind, snow flurries, and hail. Between shots, Sonnie had to lunge out from the wall to help me halt my pirouettes.

I had shot these images only five weeks prior to my diagnosis while a golf-ball-sized tumor metastasized low in my abdomen. Photographing a climb on the 350-foot spire of Monkey Face is physically intense, and as I look back, it seems even more of an accomplishment with the cancer that lurked within me.

The *Trail Runner* cover featured my friend Theresa, a waterwoman and Pilates instructor, running high above the emerald waters of Kauai, with the Nāpali Coast's lush knife-edged hills in the background. The trip to Kauai had been exactly one year before I was diagnosed with cancer.

My late friend and climbing partner Alex Newport-Berra was going to college at the University of Hawai'i, and he invited me to stay with him on Kauai for the summer. I lived on the east and south shores of the island that summer during an immensely pivotal time of growth, both personally and creatively. I was just learning to surf, but my photography career had just begun to gain some momentum, and my intuition told me there was a reason I needed to be in a place that was both visually motivating and good for the soul.

I was excited to experience the Hawaiian Islands for the first time, but also hesitant. Denali and I had not been apart for longer than a week, so leaving him for nearly two months felt almost heartrending. We had not spent more than a day or two apart since Melanie's departure. How could I ditch my best friend and biggest source of comfort for this trip? If it weren't for the quarantine and subjecting him to air travel, I would have flown with him.

One of my close friends was guiding rock climbing at Smith all summer long, and she offered to watch him while I was gone. "This trip will be so good for you," she said. "Besides, Denali loves me and he will get to spend every day with me at his favorite crag!" I hesitated, looking at Denali for assurance. "What do you think? It's your call!" He wagged his tail and seemed to almost laugh at my stress.

I'll be fine! Just come back smiling. And maybe find a nice lady who can help cheer you up. You've seemed so sad lately, no matter how hard I try to make you happy.

Kauai felt like paradise, but it was also a harsh master. The very core of my being relaxes the moment I step into a climate as temperate as Kauai, when the only articles of clothing required are board shorts and sandals, the temperature never too hot and rarely too cold. The colors of the foliage and flowers were vivid, the ocean an electric aquamarine. The island was a visual feast, and I hoped I could capture some of its beauty in my photographs.

The first morning after my arrival on the island, I paddled into a wave and was pitched suddenly by a power I was unfamiliar with, sending the nose of my eight-foot Mickey Munoz surfboard into the sand and flinging me over the tail end of the board in a tight inverted arc. While in midair, somehow my inner thigh collided with the new razor-sharp fins I had just installed, burying a trailing fin into my inner quadriceps muscle. I would never be able to repeat that unfortunate sequence of events even if I tried a thousand times.

A woman on the beach recognized the danger to my femoral artery given the proximity of the impalement and immediately applied a tourniquet for a towel as I faded into shock. After Alex tried unsuccessfully to carry me and my dysfunctional leg to his truck cab, he called an ambulance.

It was an embarrassing and painful ride to the hospital as I stared up at the local Hawaiian paramedics chuckling at a pasty white and overly stoked kid from the mainland. I learned the hard way about the power of Hawaiian waves, raw swells colliding with reefs, so different from the sandbars and point breaks of the mainland.

The emergency room doctor spent the next three hours digging sand from deep within my thigh, leaving me writhing in agony despite the painkillers. Alex had to leave the room after he nearly fainted while observing the gory spectacle. *Yo, Denali, if you're listening . . . I could really use your company about now. This really sucks!* I thought. There's nothing like being injured and in pain to appreciate the ones you care about. I really missed my furry companion and his wandering, socializing ways.

The doctor advised that I stay out of the ocean for a couple of weeks, a brutal restriction while on a tropical island surrounded by inviting waters. This limitation proved to be a blessing as we looked for alternatives to surfing. Alex suggested we spend the week of his birthday on Kalalau, a long stretch of beach that defines the tropical paradise of Kauai's north shore. Access to the beach is a stunning twelve-mile hike along the magnificent Nāpali Coast.

After years of hiking with heavy climbing and photography gear, I often joke that I hate hiking. If you want me to go on a hike, just suggest we go "explore" an area and I will gladly come along. But hiking simply for the sake of hiking, no thank you.

The Kalalau Trail is an exception. Lush greenery and gorgeous views greeted us at every turn of the trail, ripe guava and *lilikoi*, or yellow passion fruit, dangling within reach. The only thing missing was Denali trotting at my side offering his support. I was well aware of how much he would have enjoyed the hike. I laughed as I thought of sharing guava and lilikoi and lychee with him. He had an iron stomach and always ate every fruit I offered him, no matter how strange. He would have hated the heat, but within most of the valleys, the trail was shaded. It always brought me so much joy to watch the simple pleasure Denali felt when exploring new and wild places.

Alex offered to hike with the bulk of my pack's weight to keep me from aggravating my injury. He chose to hike in only flip-flops that cost a couple of dollars at the local drugstore. The cheap sandals wore out within the first seven miles, but Alex forged on without complaint, hiking the remaining distance barefoot over the lumpy kukui nut hulls that formed a cobblestone texture on the trail.

Alex and I spent the next few days exploring the beaches, foraging for fruit, and bodysurfing naked in the vast openness of the beach and emerald waters. The only clock was the sun, and we barely spoke, clicking into an easy rhythm that felt unrushed and restorative. We met two local families who had kayaked to the beach and who invited us to join them. Later, I would spend much time with many of the people I met that evening.

I was ecstatic to immerse myself into this tropical paradise, a welcome distraction from the stress I had felt about making ends meet as a freelance photographer. Living in the van kept my overhead low, but I never felt sure of when my next paycheck would arrive. Covering even the most basic living expenses was a challenge, yet I knew I had to invest in the gear I needed to work as a professional in a competitive field.

I spoke with Jane about shooting imagery for the Patagonia catalogs while on Kauai, and she promised to send me a box of clothing samples to shoot with. She had already left for vacation, and her intern forgot to send the box Jane had set aside for me. I was bummed, but knew I needed to make the most of my time in such a stunning place. I asked a few of my new friends on the island if they would be willing to work with me and asked for their sizes, then ordered a selection of apparel off the Patagonia website by charging the items to my credit card, hoping desperately that my gamble would pay off and some images would be selected for publication.

The challenges piled on, leaving me in tears, and I nearly booked an earlier flight home, but I could not afford the airfare. After my first ten days on the island, Alex decided he was too homesick to stay the full two months we had planned to spend together. He missed his girlfriend and his family back in Oregon, so he flew home. I missed Denali even more acutely, so I distracted myself by learning everything I could about surfing there, observing how the tides, swell patterns, and wind direction affected the waves. The ocean continued to punish me, but I was determined to persevere. I felt at peace while riding waves, a momentary respite from the anxieties that always haunted my psyche.

I also focused more energy on my photography, but the island seemed to delight in pushing me beyond my breaking point. My main film camera body failed after only a month into the trip, and I had no choice but to buy a replacement, a brand-new Nikon F100 body, to keep shooting. Film, processing, shipping costs, food, gasoline, and utilities were very expensive on the island, and the bills continued to pile up. To further push myself creatively and shoot beneath the waves, I decided to purchase a custom waterproof housing for my camera so I could make photographs in the ocean. Before the digital era this was a far more challenging task, as every thirty-six frames I would need to swim in, disassemble the housing, reload my camera, and make sure everything was watertight before I could swim back out and resume shooting. By the end of the summer, I was deeply committed, and $10,000 in debt from gear and expenses incurred during my stay there.

Thankfully, a voice inside shoved aside my fear of what I knew was an all-or-nothing gamble. I was at a make-or-break moment in my career, and I went all in. This island, with its rich marine colors and tropical brilliance, was the spark to create the imagery I knew I must produce to take the next step as a professional photographer. What would I fall back on if I failed and never sold another image? A life of rock climbing and adventure sport photography did not seem like a future I could make a living on, nor did it hold the depth of inspiration I sought. I had already begun to feel restless photographing climbers at their limits and started to question how I could go deeper in my work. Documenting elite athletes pushing their personal limits was satisfying to a point, but beyond meeting their own goals, did their accomplishments or my images of them affect anyone outside of our small community? Yes, they inspired others to push out of their own comfort zones, but I could not help but feel it was all so selfish in the end.

I also knew that water, especially the ocean, was an innate part of me. Surfing is magical. Afterward, the sensory overload of a challenging day begins to make sense. Bliss is found when the flow state takes over, yet the ocean is always humbling. That's why I love it.

It's a very different feeling from sending a climb or topping out on a summit . . . instead you've had the opportunity to ride a pulse of energy, formed by storms and organized by time and distance, originating hundreds or even thousands of miles away that breaks with a unique fingerprint of the sandy bottom contours and the tidal influence of the current moon phase.

No two waves are ever the same, nor are we, moment to moment.

TO FILL A NICHE CREATIVELY, I KNEW I NEEDED TO FIND MY VOICE AND STYLE. I liked the challenge of telling people's stories, getting to know them and showing the life they led beyond their peak athletic moments. While on Kauai, I photographed several female athletes in action and experimented for the first time with underwater photography. I submitted a few hundred slides from the trip to Patagonia, and Jane called me. "Ben, these are great. I never get photographs of women from the islands. Most surf photographers just send photos of women in bikinis on the beach, but you photographed them as athletes."

Wow, I thought. What kind of photographer would not shoot these beautiful women as empowered athletes? I recognized then that if I were to survive as a photographer, I would have to figure out a way to create images that would uniquely meet my clients' unfulfilled needs. A creative career is a continual evolution, and even today I consistently try to reinvent my voice. Anything less leaves me feeling bored and restless.

Fortunately, my wager worked out in the end. Before the medical bills began to accumulate, I was able to fully pay back the debts incurred from the trip. Patagonia ended up publishing images from Kauai for the following decade, paying for the trip and gear several times over. It was a solid lesson in trusting my intuition, even on a journey where everything seemed to be a challenge. Jane would later publish several full-page catalog images from Kauai during the summer that concluded my yearlong battle to survive cancer.

The reunion with Denali after that trip, after two whole months separated, was priceless. He bounded up to me, plastering my face with kisses before leaping into my lap, wriggling onto his back. As I scratched his ears and belly, he leaned into me with his eyes closed, grinning ear to ear before relaxing with a deep breath and a full-bodied sigh.

> Dude. Why'd you leave me so long? I had a blast at Smith Rock, but I really was missing you.

"I missed you, friend," I said, mirroring Denali's thoughts as I hugged him tighter. "I needed you more than anything on that trip, and I'm so glad we're together again."

5

The Diagnosis

It was June 1, 2004. I looked blearily about and saw an artificially lit room and somber expressions etched on every face. Clarity began to return sluggishly as I struggled to regain my bearings.

A voice acknowledged my stirring. "He's awake."

Explicit medical photographs were held inches from my face, images that contained an ugliness so foreign that I thought, *Surely this can't be in my body. Where the hell am I?*

Then I remembered. I had just undergone a colonoscopy, Western medicine's version of a plumber doing a full inspection of a home sewer system. This procedure is typically reserved for those passing the half-century mark of their lives. Yet I was only twenty-nine years old, a full-time rock climber and athlete in the peak years of my abilities. And this was my house, my body.

As the effects of the anesthesia slowly wore off, my surroundings became clearer. I saw the face of my roommate Byron, who had offered to give my sorry sedated ass a ride home. I studied his expression, so grim it seemed as if someone had just broken the news that his mother had died.

What's going on here? Why the long faces?

"Excuse me?" I managed to croak.

"We found a carcinoma," a faraway voice stated flatly.

A carcinoma? They most definitely are not talking about me. Even if they are referring to me, carcinoma doesn't necessarily mean cancer, does it? If it does, it must be a small tumor. And most certainly benign.

A feeling of dread began to creep through me as denial attempted to cloak my psyche.

My mind slipped for a moment as I continued to fight the aftereffects of the anesthesia, and a far-off murmuring brought me back.

"There are even women who are able to wear bikinis after a colostomy procedure . . ."

What are they even talking about this time? Sheesh, they gave me some serious sedatives, I'm definitely dreaming. This is all referring to someone else.

Studying the empty bed beside me, I slowly became aware that I was the only patient in the recovery room.

A voice continued, "Many athletes are able to wear a colostomy bag without much interruption of their activities." The male voice drew nearer, and I recognized the face of Dr. Bochner, the gastroenterologist who performed the colonoscopy.

What is a colostomy? I attempted to comprehend it all. I had never in my life heard this word before.

I thought back to Dr. Bochner's words as I was being wheeled into the procedure room. "We're just going to have a look and see what's going on in there. I doubt we'll find anything too serious, maybe just a polyp, and in that case we'll snip it out. If you have irritable bowel syndrome, we'll be able to rule out anything major." He spoke in a matter-of-fact tone, without a trace of concern. There had not been a hint of reason for alarm, no warning to help prepare me for the maelstrom of emotion and the struggle to come.

"Can someone please tell me what is going on?" I exclaimed, finally able to speak. "I don't wear bikinis and I have no idea what a colostomy is!" I glanced again at Byron for reassurance, but he averted his eyes as he grappled with the news.

Holding the images even closer, Dr. Bochner pointed to an ugly growth that resembled a deep-sea creature on the photograph. "You have colon cancer," he said. "We need to get you in immediately for an ultrasound to have your tumor staged. We could do it here in Bend, but you are so young, and this is advanced enough that I would prefer for you to have the tumor staged at Oregon Health and Science University in Portland. I want to be absolutely sure we know what you are dealing with here."

———

THE WAR HAD BEEN RAGING ON IN MY BOWELS UNTIL IT BECAME TOO EXPLOsive and bloody to ignore. I had made excuses and avoided visits to the doctor for over a year in spite of my outrageous symptoms. This denial nearly took my life.

I had met my roommate, Byron, earlier that spring while climbing at Smith Rock when Dizzy, his spastic greyhound mix, and Miles, his often-misbehaved white Lab, teamed up and harassed Denali as I lowered from a climb. "Sorry, man!" Byron said. "You mind if I take a burn on your rope?" After that day, our dogs got along well, and Byron and I became frequent climbing buddies. He knew I was living in my van, and asked if I wanted to stay with him for a few months during a rough personal spell.

A year prior, his wife had been critically injured while cycling after a car hit her at full speed. He had been fully occupied with nursing her back to health for the better part of a year, and after her full recovery, she abruptly left him.

Byron was crushed, and I could relate to some of the feelings he was grappling with. "Sure, man, I'd love to stay with you," I offered. He lived in a huge house, and I took a room in the basement so Denali and I could tuck out of the way. I gradually settled into the comfort of living in a house again, unpacking my totes and Pelican cases and setting up an office to edit photos. It was odd to not be in my van, but now that Denali and I had started sleeping in a real bed, I was leaving Big Blue parked in the driveway for days at a time.

I was single then and looking for any source of distraction from my still-undiagnosed condition. I invited a friend to go to a Ziggy Marley and Michael Franti concert. At the last minute, my friend bailed but she suggested that I invite Jeanne, a gifted Smith Rock local who was newly divorced and had just begun dating again. She was a strong rock climber who dispatched difficult 5.13 routes with ease. I had a crush on her for both her beauty and her graceful and powerful movement on the rock. Jeanne was eleven years my senior and had two young kids, two factors that gave me pause, but I thought, *What do I have to lose?* and agreed to bring her along. This decision may have saved my life.

We had fun at the show, and we started seeing each other regularly. Since I was halfway moved in with Byron but still living out of bags from my van, I stayed at her place frequently. My violent visits to the toilet were impossible to hide from her. Jeanne was a practicing chiropractor and had been married to a cardiologist, so she was familiar with the medical world. She recognized that my condition was much worse than I let on.

Jeanne asked me frankly what was going on, and I vaguely shared what I had been dealing with, embarrassed to be speaking about such personal issues. I tried to blow it off, but as I heard myself describing the symptoms, I realized how bad things had gotten. I was now carrying at least two changes of underwear with me everywhere I went. How is that normal? Fortunately, Jeanne's intuition and tact were more powerful than my deep denial, and she was able to convince me that I needed to seek help.

Jeanne offered to order a few innocent-sounding tests from the lab at the local hospital, assuring me that they were just minor to rule out parasites, anemia, and fecal blood. I was aware that I had frequent rectal bleeding, so that much was obvious, but the other tests came back negative. I felt a tentative rush of hope. Maybe my health was not as bad as my symptoms made it seem.

Jeanne still felt that something was very wrong, and her lifesaving intuition motivated her to push me further. She scheduled me an appointment with a nurse practitioner, and casually said that I should just go talk with her to put my mind at ease.

During the office visit, Gayle Riffle, the nurse practitioner, gave me my first of countless rectal exams, and sat me down afterward to tell me that she felt a mass about a finger length up my rectum. "The mass is about four centimeters up, and I am guessing that it is most likely a hemorrhoid," she said. "You probably just have irritable bowel syndrome, and could try anti-inflammatories to help you manage that, but let's get you scoped just to be sure. A sigmoidoscopy would tell us what the mass is, but I would recommend a full colonoscopy so we can see exactly what is going on."

Colonoscopy? At age twenty-nine, I was completely unfamiliar with this term.

I now realize that it was Gayle's recommendation for a colonoscopy along with Jeanne's insistence that I seek medical treatment for my ever-worsening condition that saved my life. I give credit to those two women with each breath I now take. Had I waited even a few weeks longer, I would not be alive, much less writing these words. I share this and my experience that follows in the hopes that others in my position, or those with loved ones experiencing similar symptoms, will not hesitate to get checked. The consequences are life and death, and it is better to be sure than to face the battle that I did. Colon cancer is often a slow-moving fire, smoldering in the shadows until it reaches the lymph nodes. There, overnight, the cancer explodes into a wildfire. Minor symptoms that appear to be benign suddenly evolve far beyond the tipping point, becoming metastatic tumors that rapidly spread through the stomach, liver, lungs, and brain in a matter of days.

During the two days after my colonoscopy, the seconds crawled past. My stomach was in knots as I anxiously awaited the results from the laboratory test of the tumor that had been found. Foreboding clouds poured over the Cascades, reflecting the weight of anxiety that pinned me down. My phone buzzed during a clap of thunder, and my gastroenterologist stated flatly that his suspicions had been confirmed: my tumor was indeed a malignant carcinoma.

I had CANCER. Lightning flashed, and I flinched involuntarily with the peal of thunder that followed, struggling to come to terms with my newfound reality.

Stunned, I pulled Denali close and placed my forehead on his. "Hey, D, you're the first to know this. I'm sick, Denali, really sick. I'm going to need you . . . even more than ever, okay?"

He calmly looked up at me, his eyes showing the depth of his concern. His stoic yet caring gaze was the assurance I needed that he was there for me, no matter what lay ahead.

> I got you, bro. I believe in you. You survived all that
> heartbreak and all those ladies who didn't treat you very
> nice. You can get through this too! I'm right here. Always!

My friend Jenny and I had made an agreement that if either of us texted "Code Red!" the other would reply, no matter how late the hour. The evening I was diagnosed with colon cancer, I summoned the courage to start telling my friends the surreal news.

CODE RED I typed. Even though it was one a.m., Jenny called me immediately.

"I had a colonoscopy today to figure out what was wrong with me. They think I have colon cancer. I'll know for sure in a few days," I blurted out.

"No way! You're so healthy, though!" Jenny exclaimed, trying to comprehend the drastic news of my prognosis.

The next morning, a scheduling nurse from Oregon Health and Science University phoned me, stating that the earliest available appointment for the ultrasound to stage the tumor to decide on the course of treatment would be three weeks out. *Three weeks? Every hour feels like a day. How will I last three whole weeks if I don't even know how serious this is?* I thought. Denali was glued to my side every moment between those phone calls.

You're gonna be okay! I promise. Hey, let's just go play,
okay? You always are happier when we just get outside!

I told Jeanne about the delay, and she immediately began calling
every doctor she knew and pulled every favor she had available in the
medical community until she was satisfied.

"No, he can't wait three weeks, he needs to be seen *now.*"

"They will see you in five days!" she said, a hint of a smile creeping in.

"Thank you!" I said, relieved. This act of compassion, and I imagine
intuition on her part, saved my life. Three weeks could very well have
been too late for me.

I learned then that our medical system is a cold, unfeeling machine,
and unless you have an advocate to call persistently on your behalf, or
have endless hours of energy to research and fight the system while you
battle the disease ravaging your cells, your fate will depend on the
whims of overworked specialists' schedules and, even worse, the insurance companies. Denali's constant empathy and warm friendship were
the perfect antidote to the sterile confines of the medical system. He
hated being locked inside, and I sensed that he could relate to how caged
I felt during the treatments. We had lost our freedom, of living in a
rhythm enjoying the daylight hours outside, climbing or at the beach.
Denali was restless but stayed at my side, nevertheless.

The day of my ultrasound at OHSU to stage the tumor, I was running very late, overwhelmed by Portland traffic, then confused by the
parking and labyrinthine hallways of the nearly hundred-twenty-five-
year-old buildings. The doctors at OHSU do not take kindly to waiting to perform procedures. Normally, if you are even a few minutes
late they will reschedule you and send you away without question.

The nurses at the front desk could see my desperation and over-whelmed state, and in kindness pushed me through to my appointment in spite of my being forty-five minutes late. I arrived in the room to some very pissed-off doctors, but they obliged to follow through with the procedure.

They had me lie on my right side, and I waited for them to prepare a sedative or some form of anesthesia, but that moment never came. An ultrasound wand was pushed into my rectum, and as I gritted my teeth, I sensed something was wrong. I heard the assistants say something about a malfunction as my rectum seemed to fill with air or water, I am not really sure which.

After what seemed like hours of violation, the probing paused for a moment, and I heard the doctors murmuring among themselves.

"The tumor has fully penetrated the colon wall and has reached the lymph nodes."

Pointing at the screen, one physician showed me what they were looking at.

"The tumor is right there, nearly touching the lymph nodes. You are lucky you got here in time."

The impersonal tone of his next question stunned me.

"Have you participated in a lot of anal sex? Your tumor is low in your rectum, so we wonder if there is any correlation with that and frequent anal penetration. You are so young that we are trying to understand why this happened to you."

I gasped a response. "No, the closest thing to anal I've received . . . is the wand you have inside me. And it is very uncomfortable. I don't like it. Please wrap up what you're doing in there soon. *Please!*"

The air pressure and invasion of the wand was an early experience in my treatment with the impersonal nature that is so pervasive in Western medicine. Doctors and nurses are so overworked that they have little reserve for empathy. Fluorescent lights, cold tile, IV drips, and beeping EKGs and blood oxygen sensors leave little space for the calm our bodies and minds need to heal.

After doctors staged the tumor at OHSU in Portland, I began the most challenging summer of my life, with nearly daily radiation and chemotherapy treatment before surgery to remove the tumor three months later. My relationship with Denali deepened even further that summer as he doubled down on his role as my primary caretaker, confidant, and best friend.

———

I DID MY BEST TO PROCESS THE NEWS THAT THE ROGUE CELLS WITHIN MY body indeed formed a malignant and cancerous tumor. It was disconcerting, but it also felt oddly comforting to finally identify the alien forces that had been tearing me apart from within.

A few hours passed, and my cell phone rang, an old rowing buddy from my college crew team calling to chat. He was beside himself with excitement and wanted to share the news that he had qualified in the Olympic trials for the men's pair event. I mustered enough energy to congratulate him on the honor, suppressing laughter at the morbid irony of the timing of his call. "How are you doing, man? It's been a while," he asked.

"Well, today I got the news . . . um, I was diagnosed with colon cancer. It sounds bad," I answered, feeling numb and detached from my voice.

The line was silent, and I sat wondering how he would respond. I heard a click from the other end, followed by a "beep . . . beep . . . beep." He had hung up on me.

His reaction was cold and unfeeling, yet I somehow understood. He was single-mindedly focused on a goal: to make the 2004 Summer Olympics. His inability to comprehend the mortal battle I now faced was simply due to the selfish pursuit of athletic excellence.

I realized that I, too, needed to face this disease with this same single-minded focus. Survival mode, locked in, no room for doubt or self-pity. I could show no mercy . . . these rogue cells must die. My life depended on it.

Denali lay in my lap as I pondered my situation for the next few hours. I decided to phone Jane Sievert, my photo editor and mentor at Patagonia. Her time was in high demand, and Jane was rarely available for much more than a three-minute call, if she even answered the phone. I told her I might not be able to shoot for her very much over the next few months because I was sick, basically sharing that my photo career was taking a back seat until I knew whether I would live or die. Jane surprised me by staying on the line for nearly an hour, offering love, encouragement, and support. She assured me that the photo team and the Patagonia family would be there for anything I might need.

Six months later, still healing from painful surgeries, burned from radiation, weak from chemo, I drove with Denali to spend Thanksgiving with Jane and a few other Patagonia friends in the old-growth redwoods of Northern California. That time outside with Denali and among loving friends helped me recover and feel more grounded. It was an essential step in preparing me for the eight rounds of chemo that lay ahead.

Cancer is brutal, indiscriminate of both priorities and relationships. All focus goes to survival, and you cannot afford to spend emotional energy to understand why some of your friends rise to the occasion and others simply avoid facing the unnatural reality of the disease. If a seemingly healthy athlete in his twenties could be diagnosed with this disease, one typically associated with those in their last third of life, how could they feel assured of the immortality of youth?

During my encounter with cancer, supportive friendships emerged from the most unlikely places, and others evaporated within moments of my diagnosis. I lacked the energy to even acknowledge those friends who chose to step aside and disappear. All that remained was the resolve to live, which meant I needed to commune with those who embraced life. Through all the turmoil and confusion of this prolonged battle, there was one friend who never wavered, and always had my back. He kept me in touch with my dirtbag self, always reminding me of my need to be outside. His name was Denali.

6

The Battle

In the months following my appointment with the nurse practitioner, it seemed every doctor had a contract stating that they were required to manually examine my tumor, meaning rubber gloves and a finger up my butthole. It started feeling oddly automatic to voluntarily drop my pants to my ankles, then lean on the exam table and try to disassociate from the discomfort and intrusion.

The oncologist who managed my treatment was the first to say, "No, I don't need to do that."

I was so ecstatic to hear his words that I nearly gave him a huge hug. This was the beginning of my long and positive relationship with Dr. Braich, a collaborative effort to keep me alive. He was matter-of-fact, "drier than a martini," as a fellow doctor described him, yet he was empathetic and caring. Those are challenging characteristics to maintain in the world of cancer, where many patients lose their battle with the very disease he is helping them fight against.

Looking back now, I am not sure I was ever fully aware how serious my prognosis was. *I'm only stage II . . . yet they're treating me as if I'm stage IV. It must just be because I'm young and they think I can handle it*, I thought. But, in colorectal cancer, the time frame and prognosis that differentiates stage II from stage IV is paper thin. The cells advance slowly, methodically, for months or even years, and you may be symptom-free. And then just days later, the mutation invades the lymph nodes and, suddenly, it is too late.

Dr. Braich recommended that I immediately start radiation treatments to shrink the tumor, while simultaneously beginning a chemotherapy regimen administered 24-7 by a portable chemo pump, a device the size of a VHS tape that made an ominous whirring sound, finishing with a "kerrr-thunk" every ten minutes while it squirted another dose of poison into my circulatory system.

The chemo was pumped through thin plastic tubing called a peripherally inserted central catheter, or PICC line, which entered through the large vein in my inner arm, where a junkie would shoot up. Only instead of the escape of a euphoric high, I was left nauseated and sucked of my will to exist.

In the heat of that Bend summer, I was not allowed to enter the water for fear of infection. I have never liked the heat much, and am always drawn to swimming holes or the ocean whenever temperatures crest eighty degrees Fahrenheit. Being prohibited from immersing myself in water was pure torture during those three long months, and it made me recognize how essential those moments of immersion are for my well-being.

This was one more reminder of how drastically different my life was now. I often threw the ball for Denali at the river's edge, living vicariously through him as he dove after it into the icy snowmelt. Seeing his pleasure made me feel less like I was missing out.

Clear Tegaderm bandages covered the insertion point where the tubing disappeared into my arm. The area was red with Betadine antiseptic and the irritated skin underneath. Later in the summer, I noticed the PICC line was slowly working its way out of my arm, becoming longer and longer at the surface. The nurse who originally placed it seemed distracted and had hurried through the process, asking few questions before inserting a thicker version of the line. Unfortunately, he did not take my activity level into consideration, even though I shared that I was an avid rock climber and mountain biker.

While my PICC line and chemo pump were being set up, I visited the radiation oncology department to have the treatment calibrated to the tumor location and my body size. The meticulous preparations for the treatments had included tattooing me with a greenish-blue dot of ink on each hip to ensure that the tumor was precisely targeted. Lead molds were made to guide the radioactive particles to penetrate deep into my pelvic cavity, where the tumor was hiding within my bowels.

The morning I was scheduled for my first radiation treatment, I was discussing the procedure with the oncologist when a radiation therapist named Christy burst into the oncologist's office. "Dr. Comerford!" she exclaimed. "Ben is only twenty-nine years old! He might want to have kids someday. We need to make sure we let him have that opportunity." Up until Christy's well-timed realization, they had planned to nuke me with my balls lying naked between my thighs, which would have ghosted my future generations with the first blast of protons.

As the initial protocol didn't account for protecting my reproductive capability, the machine now needed to be recalibrated to make space between my legs for an unsophisticated protective device that amounted to an ill-fitting lead clamshell for my testicles. In the facility's haste to correct the error and get me back on schedule, I had to borrow the nut shield from a previous patient. The fit was not generous. It was like using custom orthotics that weren't made for you, or a pair of Rainbow flip-flops or Birkenstock sandals that another foot had molded over years and miles of walking.

Intent on protecting my reproductive capacities, I dutifully stuffed the errant folds of scrotal skin that always seemed to get pinched into the hollowed-out lead armor. The imposing robotic arm wound around my prone body in an eight-foot radius. Every ninety degrees it would pause, emitting an audible buzz as it shot invisible radioactive particles into my torso. The whole experience was intimidating, requiring an internal argument to convince myself to lie there for each of the twenty-eight treatments.

Christy would stand outside the room and ask if I was doing okay as I lay facedown on the cold vinyl of the narrow platform, grunting and wrestling to tuck all the skin into the small device without pinching my scrotum. The only place I lost my hair during any chemo or radiation was around my ass and tender bits. I was like a prepubescent teenager down there. Some people pay good money for laser hair removal, and I was literally hair-free after the first few treatments, leaving everything baby smooth.

"How's everything looking today?" I would ask as she inspected the condition of my skin. I don't think there is a more awkward and vulnerable feeling than lying strapped to a table with your ass spread apart, while a beautiful woman scrutinizes the skin around your anus.

My other radiation therapists were named Greg and Vivi, a couple who climbed at Smith Rock and had a cat that hung out in their Volkswagen camper. Along with Christy, they would chat with me during the sessions, adding welcome empathy to my care and helping to humanize an entirely unnatural experience.

After my radiation dosing, I would walk across the street from the St. Charles Cancer Center to the small building across the street where they would recharge my chemotherapy pump with fluorouracil, nicknamed "5-FU," a drug commonly used to treat bowel, breast, and stomach cancer. I often thought it meant saying "F-you" to cancer five times over.

When I returned home after each treatment, Denali would greet me eagerly. He was reserved, being careful not to be too rough with my compromised and battered body. We would lie on my roommate's expansive leather couch, Denali's back pressed against me while we watched Lance Armstrong dominate the 2004 Tour de France. I often fell asleep to the rhythm of the peloton, only waking up after four or five hours had passed.

Byron would usually attempt to coax me out for a bike ride and, to avoid the summer heat and dust, we often opted to bike on the scenic roads outside Bend, the tubes of my PICC line flapping in the wind. Other cyclists would pass us and ask, "What's in the bag?" to which I would retort, "I'm juicing on EPO, what do you expect? Do you want some?"

When it was cool enough to bike the trails just west of Bend, we could take Denali and Dizzy and Miles, Byron's two dogs. We would all leave from Phil's Trailhead, winding through the ponderosa pines on dusty single-track circuits in the foothills of the Cascade Range. Those moments on the trail were exhilarating, allowing both Denali and me to escape the confines of the treatment schedule, the rush of speed and dusty air in our faces providing a temporary release from the gravity of my diagnosis.

During the first few weeks of treatment, I tried to bike and climb often. I did not realize that each time I bent my arm, the PICC line tubing was rolling and twisting in the vein that delivered it to my heart. I mentioned to my doctor that it seemed the tubing was slowly working itself out of my body, and pointed out the extra tubing that was coiled in the crook of my arm.

He ordered an ultrasound to see how much of the tubing remained, and discovered a blood clot in my upper arm. The tubing was pulled, and a thinner, more flexible PICC line was inserted, this time on the inside of my upper arm, a much more comfortable position. Because of the blood clot, daily Lovenox injections into my abdomen were added to my daily lap of doctor visits on the sprawling campus of medical buildings located on both sides of the street. These shots felt like a wasp's sting, but I resigned myself to the procedure. It was just another battlefront in the prolonged assault on the rogue cells residing within me.

My friend Katie Brown was visiting Bend on an extended climbing trip at Smith Rock, just twenty-five minutes north of the city. She was a professional rock climber who at one time was one of the most well-known female climbers in the world. Soon after her arrival in the area, Katie noticed that I did not have a lot of support or family nearby and asked if she could crash in the spare bedroom at Byron's. I am not sure that I fully comprehended this gesture then, as I was too focused on my own survival. I thought Katie just wanted to stay in town because of the proximity to the climbing at Smith Rock.

I was grateful for her kind presence, and by simply being there for me, she helped lift me out of a few of my darkest moments. I dislike asking for help or burdening anyone, but I knew for certain that I could not handle having my mother hovering over me. I believed that with Denali at my side, and with Byron upstairs, I would be fine, but Katie's intuition that I needed a friend was a major factor in my healing process that summer.

Katie shared recently that at the time, she felt unable to help me with words, so she thought that by staying with me she would help out any way she could. She was surprised by how chill I seemed with it all.

I felt like anyone else would have been angry or pissed off . . . or a total train wreck," she said. "But it seemed to me that you were so calm with it all, like there was no doubt that it would get better. Because to me you didn't seem to waver or be like, 'I can't believe this is happening to me,' or anything negative. You just seemed to be very even keel and positive and [had] moved on to taking the next steps that needed to happen. You just rolled with it, which was the crazy thing that stuck out to me. Which I'm sure it didn't seem like internally to you, but externally to me that's what it seemed like.

One morning I was resting at home, recovering from the latest rounds of radiation, and Katie made the caring gesture to bring me tea while I was still in bed, handing the hot beverage to me in my favorite insulated mug. I realized the lid was on backward, so I tried to twist it back into place and instead flicked the lid onto my chest. I let out a yelp as hot steam trapped under the lid scalded my chest. Katie felt awful, but I knew her intentions came from a place of compassion.

That evening, my friend David Kottkamp, a badass athlete then in his early sixties who always invited me on cycling rides and adventures in the snow and surf, invited us over to his house to watch a surf film from the eighties. As I took off my jacket, David asked me how the treatments were going and then pointed to my chest. "Is the radiation making you all swollen?" he said jokingly.

I laughed and said, "No, why?" then realized my shirt was indeed puffed up near my sternum. Lifting my shirt revealed a huge blister from where the tea had scalded me that morning. I had been dealing with so many other discomforts from the treatments that I had not even noticed. "Whoa," Katie said, "I'm so sorry!"

"Katie tried to assassinate me!" I teased. "Or were you trying to kill me with kindness?" We continued to laugh through the evening as we watched *North Shore*, a Hollywood surf movie that starred Gerry Lopez, Laird Hamilton, and other professional surfers and was hilarious in its exaggerated earnestness to portray surf culture. During treatment, it was vital that I laugh with friends. Humor and optimism kept me from slipping into the void of feeling sorry for myself, and Denali made sure I never felt alone.

My radiation treatments continued, and I was physically managing them quite well, but psychologically they took a toll. I counted out the sessions that remained, and realized I had made it about two-thirds through the regimen. The doctors had given me a Friday off, and I relished a day away from that dreaded concrete radiation room.

I felt good enough to run a few errands, so I checked my post office box for the first time in weeks and then took my mail and headed to the laundromat for a much-needed cleansing of my wardrobe. I tossed my stained puffy jackets and clothes matted with Denali's hair and Smith Rock's volcanic dust into an oversized washer, then sat down to open a heavy rectangular package the mail clerk had held for me behind the counter.

Inside, atop a two-inch-thick ream of documents, was a check made out to Benjamin Moon, for over $1,200. *Wow, a refund?* I thought. *Bonus!*

Setting the check aside, I pulled out the cover letter on top and noticed it was from American Family Insurance. I had used them for my auto insurance policies for years, so I wondered if they were giving me some odd bonus for good driving or had made a mistake in my favor on my premiums.

Just weeks prior to my cancer diagnosis, I knew deep down something was wrong—very wrong with me. I called my insurance agent, whom I knew quite well from auto insurance claims over the past few years. I asked him if adding health insurance coverage to my policy was a possibility. I was walking a slackline, steadying myself as I balanced on one foot and raising my free arm as I chatted with him on my old Motorola flip phone. He confirmed that the coverage had been added as I walked, not realizing that a tumor the size of a racquetball was growing through the side of my rectum, cells multiplying out of control as it marched toward my lymph nodes.

Unfortunately, the refund was not a kind gesture, it was quite the contrary. My coverage was being rescinded because of a preexisting condition when I signed up for the policy. My cancer diagnosis had set their underwriters into full detective mode, scouring my records until they found mention in my gastroenterologist's notes that I had seen blood in my stool the year prior to my policy start date. Their work was done, and they unceremoniously dumped me from the policy. When I returned to the house, Denali sensed my defeat.

Hey, man, what's going on?! You'll get through this. We'll figure it out, and besides, no matter what happens I've got your back!

The insurance company was heartless, using corporate tactics to shirk risk and responsibility. This very well could have caused me financial ruin, but laziness or maybe a subconscious intuition had prevented me from canceling the inexpensive health insurance policy that I had signed up for the previous year. Even on my aspiring photographer's meager income, the monthly forty-eight-dollar automatic payment on the catastrophic policy was barely enough to notice on my bank statements for the first few months. The catastrophe I never expected had indeed happened, and my laissez-faire approach in dealing with "life matters" was a blessing in this case and saved me from bankruptcy.

Even though I was still nervous about paying for my medical and living expenses, the initial shock of being dumped from my insurance had subsided. I was taking the situation one day at a time as I neared the end of my radiation regimen. I went in for the twenty-fifth of my twenty-eight radiation treatments, but Dr. Comerford wisely advised I take break from the daily dosing for a couple of days to allow my skin to heal. I was determined to get the treatments over with, so I challenged his advice. "I am fine!" I said, adamant to continue. "There is almost no sensitivity down there." The doctor obliged, but unfortunately for me, I soon realized that I should have listened to him.

After the day's treatment, I sat on the toilet and felt an excruciating pain that I can only describe as glass shards shredding my bowels as they cartwheeled down through my colon into my rectum. Tears were streaming down my face as I passed my breaking point. I cried out in agony, letting out an unearthly wail. Denali, ever attentive to my compromised condition, had been waiting for me just outside the bathroom door. With a determined shove of his strong head and neck, he forced open the latched bathroom door. He looked up at me with concerned eyes. I'll do anything for you. Just say the word and I'll make it all go away. Curling tenderly around my feet, he tried to get as close to me as he could. Still clenched in pain, my hands finally relaxed enough that I could reach down to scratch his ears, my heart welling in gratitude. "Thank you, Nali. You've seen me at my lowest, and this isn't over yet. I'm going to need you more than ever in the days ahead. I love you, buddy."

———

WHILE I BATTLED CANCER, WHAT I CRAVED MORE THAN ANYTHING WERE THE healing waters of the ocean.

I was born in New Orleans and raised near the shores of Lake Michigan, so I have a visceral need for water. The ocean especially, as it is always grounding and a humbling reminder of my smallness within the universe.

When I was a child, we took the Amtrak train to visit my grandparents in Colorado's Front Range, and I recall tugging on Mom's sleeve as we walked near a large reservoir and asking her, "Where's the water, Mom?"

During my cancer treatments, friends and clients helped facilitate surf trips to Mexico and Kauai that enabled me to recharge and heal. One such trip was during the three "off" weeks the doctors granted me between radiation treatments and the surgery to remove my tumor. At the suggestion of Jane, my photo editor at Patagonia, I flew to the south shore of Kauai with Lisa B, a good friend of mine from Bishop. She was a talented rock climber, surfer, and yoga instructor who had been crippled by the symptoms of her recent rheumatoid arthritis diagnosis. Lisa was undergoing chemotherapy treatments to reduce the inflammation that was rendering her joints useless to the point where she could barely turn a doorknob.

It was easy to convince Lisa to make the hike into Kalalau, the beach I had visited with Alex the year before my diagnosis. She and I had agreed to stop and make camp at the six-mile mark, a halfway point that broke up the hike into a more casual venture. The rain fell nonstop as we wound our way through lush valleys, scenic overlooks, and stream crossings.

My skin was tender when we set out, and by the time we pitched the tent, I was convinced the skin around my anus was shredding with every step. Setting aside any shame, I asked Lisa if she could please inspect the tender region to make sure I did not need medical attention.

Being a dear friend, she bravely obliged. Setting aside my ego once again, I dropped my board shorts and braced for the bad news, sure that my guts had fallen out my ass. "You have a cute butthole. It's mostly bald and all your hair that's left is blond!" she exclaimed. "You're all good down there." Relieved, I thanked her and got ready for bed, happy that my rearward parts were still intact.

The following evening, it was still pouring as we arrived at the exposed red-dirt section of the trail. It was usually my favorite portion of the hike, but the rain had made the clay soil utterly treacherous. Mud built up inside and beneath my Chaco sandals, sucking my feet underground and sliding with each step forward. We literally clawed our way on hands and knees, using sticks for self-arrest anchors as we traversed the steep hillside. Five hundred feet below us, the Pacific Ocean churned with swell, reminding us of our fate if we made a misstep. Finally, at dusk the rain eased, and we arrived at the open beach near the cave where we planned to sleep.

My rear end was in agony, and all I could think of was to get in the ocean to ease the discomfort. Barely glancing at the state of the ocean, I dove headlong into the waves crashing near the shore and swam toward the open horizon. The burning sensation down under dramatically escalated as my tender skin made contact with salt water just as I realized that the swell was significantly larger than I had realized. The pain in my ass sharply gave way to the sobering fact that in order to return to dry sand, I needed to navigate a head and a half (a nine-foot) wave without ending up with a spinal injury. I waited for a lull between sets of waves and allowed the force of a smaller wave to shove me back onto the beach. Now my tender ass was not only salty but also packed with sand. Sighing with resignation to my plight, I chuckled and glanced over at Lisa, who had been wide eyed with worry a few moments before.

We jokingly called ourselves Team Gimp, the two chemo patients who were broken from both disease and heartbreak, on a trip that we both needed as a reset. Lisa and I embraced our deficiencies, surfing longboards on the tiny peeling waves at a left-reef point break near where we were staying, arriving at sunrise to watch the locals carve graceful lines and lounge about on their boards as they laughed and spoke in their native Hawaiian Pidgin dialect. Looking back, I'm not sure I appreciated the fact that this would be my last time wearing board shorts slung low without a colostomy bag showing over my waistband.

One day at sunset, near the end of our time on Kauai, I was shooting lifestyle images for Patagonia, wandering tide pools along the south shore reefs with Lisa B. I was crouched at the edge of a tide pool in my usual *malasana* squatting position, lining up a shot, when my Rainbow sandals lost traction, sending me, my Nikon F5 camera, and the 15 mm fish-eye lens into the salty pool. I tried to hold the camera above water, but my ass hit the reef first and the whiplash drove my arms downward, dunking my big camera. I immediately pulled the battery but smelled burning electrical circuitry and knew it was a goner.

I had purchased my first camera, the Nikon N90s, in 2000 when newspapers were ditching their film cameras for the new ease of digital. My clients were much slower to convert to digital, and the sensors in the early professional digital camera bodies were only about eight megapixels, cost $8,000 new, and had an image quality that is easily outperformed today by the current iPhone models.

Many of the images I produced during my illness and radiation and chemotherapy rounds lacked a spark, and often felt flat and uninspired. Yet through it all, my clients in the outdoor industry supported me and kept my career alive. Especially Patagonia. From day one of my diagnosis, they were more than a client, they were family. With their support, my morale stayed high enough to continue to pick up my camera.

Tanned and surfed out after my healing trip to Kauai, I went to see Dr. Higgins for a pre-op checkup, ready to get the invasive tumor out of my system. He declared me healthy enough for the procedure, and a few days later, I was being wheeled to the operating room by the surgical assistant. I was well aware of the risks of the surgery due to my cancerous rectum's proximity to the nerve bundles that controlled the muscles for urination and erectile function. Dr. Higgins had warned me that there was a fifty-fifty chance that I would be impotent following the surgery. I was not even thirty years old, and the idea of not being able to have a simple boner was horrifying even though this surgery was necessary to save my life.

The last words I spoke before the anesthesia wrapped me into its void were directed at Dr. Higgins. I looked him in the eye and said, "Be careful in there, I don't want to need a Viagra sponsorship."

———

AS MY ROOM AT ST. CHARLES MEDICAL CENTER SLOWLY CAME INTO FOCUS, my assisting surgeon and climbing friend Dr. Azin sat quietly at my bedside. He leaned in and gently assured me that the surgery had gone remarkably well, and added that they had not only removed the cancerous tumor from my rectum but also repaired an umbilical hernia and removed my swollen appendix, which was on the verge of bursting. "A three-for-one deal!" he exclaimed. "And just so you know, your other guts looked great. Here's a few photos if you want to see."

I was feeling optimistic and surprisingly pain-free and began calling and emailing friends to share the good news.

I called the Patagonia photo department and spoke with Jeff Johnson (then a staff photographer, now best known for his role in the *180° South* documentary). I told him the surgery was a success and I was feeling great. My enthusiasm was short-lived, as the doctors decided it would be fine to remove my epidural. I suddenly felt *everything.* The pain was so intense that I was barely able to sit, much less stand, my muscles too weak from the long incision that had split my abdomen in two. The intensity of it all caused my spirits to deteriorate rapidly.

Discouragement began to shadow my optimism until Denali strolled into my room. My mom and a nurse had sneaked him in. He intently locked eyes with me to reassure me he would never again leave my side. Denali sat down at the side of the bed, tail thumping slowly on the tile floor. He watched me closely, awaiting an invitation. "Of course, buddy, you're always welcome next to me," I said, calling him up with a pat of my hand.

Denali leaped up on the sheets with grace, carefully avoiding the tangle of IV lines and blood oxygen sensors. Studying me with a concerned look, he once again asked if he could come nearer. I invited him to come closer, and he lay down as if in slow motion, gently curling up against my side. The awareness and care he showed in that moment would be repeated countless times in the weeks and months to come. I felt loved and supported in a way that is indescribable.

Jenny was one of my first visitors after the doctors pulled my epidural, and seeing her caring face helped dull the intensity of the pain from my incision. Jenny recently shared a few memories of that time:

> When I first saw you in the hospital, you were in a gown, and your butt was totally wrapped in gauze. You were super skinny, and Denali was right there beside you. He was so gentle getting up on the bed.
>
> Denali *knew* not to jump on you in the hospital bed. Just sat right next to you and looked up at you real worried and concerned. It was soooo sweet.
>
> It was such a different scene to see you like that, because you were such an athlete and so full of life. You know, climbing, surfing—you had this life that I really envied, and all of a sudden you were fragile, and your butt-butt had just gotten stitched up.
>
> We had no idea what your life would be after that. You weren't yourself and everything was just unknown . . . you felt super burdened by the medical bills and what your life

was going to be like. You didn't have a girlfriend, so you were worried about what it would be like to date again. Our friend Julio had talked to you about his own struggle after colon cancer surgery and how long his sexual function took to come back again.

You were single and feeling really lonely, and I just felt kind of bad for you.

———

INITIALLY, I HARDLY HAD THE STRENGTH TO SIT UPRIGHT, AND SHAWNDI, A friend who was also a physical therapist from another department in the hospital, began to visit me a couple of times a day to help me sit, then stand, and then take a few hesitant steps. A few days later, I finally was able to complete one full lap around the halls of my hospital floor. I gave her a big hug and told her, "I think I can get through this, thank you so much, Shawndi."

Toward the end of my hospital stay, I mysteriously lost my ability to urinate. I wheeled my IV stand to the bathroom and stood unsteadily at the toilet, holding one hand under warm water in the sink and the other in the hot shower, staring down at my stubborn penis. I verbally entreated my bladder to release its voluminous contents.

As I visualized waterfalls and flowing rivers, I finally pushed my call button and begged the nurse for a catheter. I watched in horror as she lubed the end of the sixteen-inch tube and then slid it into the tip of my penis, up my urethra, until it reached my stretched bladder and the urine began to flow. My discomfort shifted to sweet relief as the pressure diminished. My odd moment of ecstasy was interrupted as the nurse exclaimed, "Oh my," as she carefully handled the receptacle that nearly overflowed with two liters of my piss.

Her face deadpan, the nurse joked, "Wow, you really had to go."

"I wasn't joking," I retorted. "Do you think I would ask for a catheter unless I was absolutely desperate?"

Never in my life had I experienced such odd discomfort and desperation as when I was unable to empty a full bladder.

Due to my inability to urinate, Dr. Higgins recommended I take another trip into the impersonal cylinder of the CT scanner. As I emerged from the test, he told me the scan had shown that an infected abscess had taken over the void left by the removal of my rectum, putting pressure on the nerves that controlled my bladder function.

A procedure was arranged to insert a Jackson-Pratt (JP) drain into the infected surgical site. A JP drain is essentially plastic tubing that pulls fluid from the problem area and into a grenade-shaped bulb that is squeezed before insertion to form a suction, keeping the wound site dry to combat infection.

A week later, I had worked back up to walking laps around the hospital floors, and with the infection seemingly under control, my doctors released me to go home. I was ecstatic. Looking at Denali, I said, "Hey, Nali, where do you want to go hike?" I just wanted to breathe fresh air and be anywhere other than the antiseptic institutional hallways from the past couple of weeks.

A FEW WEEKS AFTER THE MAJOR SURGERY TO REMOVE MY TUMOR, BYRON WAS hosting a barbecue party, and I went inside to pee and . . . could not.

No. This can't be happening again, I thought.

I willed my bladder to unload its contents. I pleaded. I concentrated with every ounce of will, focusing my energy to my abdomen. Hopping in the bathtub I let the warm water from the shower cascade over me and prayed the warmth would relax my muscles and allow my bladder to release.

My determined efforts were to no avail, so I dressed and went outside with Denali and Miles, Byron's Lab, and dialed Dr. Higgins's mobile number.

"Hey, man, I can't pee again."

"Oh no! Sorry to hear that, Ben. I know you don't want to hear this, but there could be another infection, so you need to come in right away. Are you able drive yourself?"

"*Miles, no!*" I yelled as he tried to stick his face into the hot barbecue.

"Oh wow, yes, *no*, oh no," I said as I felt hot urine streaming down my leg.

"I'm peeing! See you soon, Andy!" I shouted into the phone as I ripped open my pants and felt sweet relief.

I sped to the hospital, checked in, and immediately was put in the intensive care unit. My nurse was a climber I had seen at the gym and had a minor crush on. "Hi, good to see you," I said awkwardly. "I don't want to be here, at all . . . but I think my infection came back."

"I'll take good care of you," she said as she hooked up my IV and affixed the adhesive EKG pads to my chest, and the machines beeped and whirred and lights flashed. It wasn't even remotely dark as I tried to sleep after hearing they had scheduled my surgery for the following morning.

"You still awake?" my nurse asked. "You have visitors."

Katie walked in with Byron and Adam Stack, another pro climber and friend.

"I brought you crepes," she said, "with blueberry filling!"

Earlier that morning, Katie had asked what my favorite food was, and I told her that I had been craving my birthday breakfast treat growing up, Swedish pancakes with cherry and blueberry filling.

I almost broke into tears as gratitude overtook me. "Thank you," I managed to croak. "Thank you so much. I'm so glad you came. I hate being in here again. This room is awful and loud and bright. Hospitals are the loneliest places."

They all came over and hugged me. "No worries. We want to be here."

During surgery, the doctors cut me back open to clean out the infected abscess in the space where my rectum used to be, and Dr. Higgins placed drains from that space out through the ghost of my butthole. The drains were made of a material similar to a TheraBand, but in inch-and-a-half-wide hollow tubes pinched flat and running parallel to my ass crack. These tubes allowed my abscess to drain through my late, great anus, so my body could heal from the inside out, where my rectum used to be.

Once more, I swallowed my pride and left my dignity at the door, and I shopped for packages of maxipads, lining my underwear to catch the bodily fluids that leaked out through my temporary drainage system.

A few days after I was released from intensive care, I needed to move my body in spite of being doped up on opiates to combat the waves of pain from the freshly reopened incision. I met up with a climbing and photographer buddy named Dan to go skate some hills on my longboard. We found a new subdivision under construction on the outskirts of Bend that had brand-new pavement but no traffic whatsoever. Dan was shooting photographs as I tried to reconnect with my body as I skated. As I passed by him, I alternated nose rides with breaking traction on the wheels and sliding past him in low carves.

I took one pass at speed, my wheels preemptively breaking loose on a patch of pine needles, causing me to dramatically wipe out. As I skidded to a halt on the pavement, I caught my right butt cheek and tugged excruciatingly on my fresh incision. The agony pierced my druggy fog of postsurgical painkillers, and it felt like I might have literally ripped myself a new asshole. Fortunately, I did not.

The benefit auction that my friends had been helping me put together to help with my bills was held just days after my surgery to address the abscess. I had been walking around Bend carrying a foam cushion everywhere I went, as sitting was more painful than standing.

The help I received from outdoor companies like Patagonia and Prana was beyond generous, and there was so much gear donated for the auction that it literally filled up an entire spare bedroom at Byron's from floor to ceiling.

In the predawn hours on the morning of the event, Kelly and Joi, two of my close climbing friends from Bishop, showed up at my place and phoned from the driveway. I invited them in and hugged them both for a long time, absorbing all the love like a dry sponge. "Thank you so much for coming all this way!" I said, grateful but still exhausted. I told them I needed to sleep a bit more, and they asked if it was okay for them to be there with me. I lay down to rest, and they simply held me from either side for the next few hours with Denali curled up in the middle of it all. I absorbed every ounce of their care in those quiet moments, desperately needing the kindness and energy of my friends during that time.

I still doubted that anyone would show up to the party that night and was weak and in pain from that second surgery for my infection, so when nearly four hundred people, many of them my heroes in the climbing and photography world, showed up and raised nearly $35,000 to put toward my medical bills, I was astounded by the support. It was a massive outpouring of love, and it filled the lonely void I had been feeling since my surgery. Even though there were at least five professional photographers there, I do not have a single photograph from that night, but the feeling of that support still remains.

The next day, everyone who was staying with me went home, their focus shifting back to their everyday routines. In my weakened state, I was unable to cope with that sudden transition of hundreds of hugs and words of encouragement one moment to simply nothing the next. I felt a loneliness I had never experienced before, like a light switch had been slammed to the off position. I lay there feeling sorry for myself, doubting I would ever have a girlfriend and craving any sort of validation that I was worthy of love. Just as I was feeling that the loneliness was too much, Denali hopped onto the bed and gently laid his head on my chest. I'm still here his eyes spoke to me as they radiated his support. "I need you more than ever now," I told him. "This is harder than I could ever imagine."

I was chatting recently with Jenny about how I felt the morning after my benefit, and she recalled a few insights she had during that experience.

> Your benefit auction was a really fun party, but that night you told me, "I just really need to snuggle with somebody." I saw that everybody loved you, and I thought you were kind of a big deal and kind of famous, but the morning after the party, I just remember you were super sad and seemed so lonely . . . even though you seemed to have a million people who loved you.

I occupied myself by going through the cards and items left over from the auction. Chris Malloy, a professional surfer and filmmaker, had donated several surf films to the benefit and signed a copy of his sixteen-millimeter surf film *Shelter* for me.

On the DVD jacket he wrote, "You can do anything."

This was a quote from the film by his then-sixteen-year-old cousin—now a prominent commercial director—Britt Caillouette, who had just survived bone cancer, his leg amputated right above the knee. It was Britt's first time out surfing since his treatment, and he was really nervous about getting back into the ocean. With the help of his two cousins Keith and Dan Malloy supporting him on either side, he tossed his crutches down the beach and said, "You can do anything." It is such a touching scene, and I watched the film repeatedly throughout my chemo treatment until I knew nearly every line.

One part I always loved was Rob Machado saying, "Jon Swift is an astrophysicist," while playing a song on the guitar, before the film cuts to a scene of Jon finding solitude in the surf.

After the benefit event and three weeks out from my second surgery, I felt I had healed enough to climb a bit out at Smith Rock. After a few easy warm-ups, I sat staring up at the overhanging arête known to rock climbers and adventure photographers alike as Chain Reaction, a climb that is rated 5.12c and is so picturesque that it has graced the covers of countless magazines. I love the movement of the climb, and I impulsively asked if I could get a belay and see how it would feel. I managed to climb through the challenging lower moves and clipped the quickdraw at the lip of the steep forty-five-degree profile.

The final crux move is a big throw requiring a lot of body tension in order to keep both feet on the overhanging wall, but my abdomen had been literally split in two by the surgeries, so the muscles were incredibly weak. Just a few weeks earlier, even sitting upright was exhausting. I could not maintain the necessary tension to connect my feet to the wall, and both slipped away, leaving my legs dangling as I held on to the corner of the arête with my right hand and a large "jug" hold with my left. I tried repeatedly to swing my feet to the wall, but my abdominals were completely unresponsive. I simply wavered in the air, like a wind sock being whispered to by a gentle breeze.

I dropped onto the rope in resignation. "Lower me," I hollered down.

I rested for an hour, then knew I had to give it one more attempt. This time I climbed smoothly up to the same section of the climb, moving fluidly and wasting very little energy. As I reached the lip, I latched firmly onto the pinch with my right hand, and placed my feet deliberately, pressing hard to avoid slipping off. Instead of engaging my useless core muscles, I gyrated my hips to work each foot firmly onto the footholds so they would have maximum purchase on the rock.

Pressing hard with both legs, I sagged my weakened torso and launched into the air. I latched onto the big hold, and after my feet flung backward, I used the return swing to carefully match my left heel to my left hand. Rocking my weight over that foot, I pushed downward and pulled into the final moves and to the anchor until I was standing on the same flat handhold I had thrown myself to.

I was ecstatic to have completed the climb. *I'm back*, I thought. *I faced the challenge of surgery and still can actually climb! Colostomy bag and all*. Denali gave me a nudge and licked my salty arms in an affirming gesture.

My friends all gave me hugs of encouragement, but it was the quiet comment of a climber I did not know who had observed both of my ascents and asked a few questions about my cancer battle. "That was one of the most inspiring things I've ever witnessed," she said.

Me? Inspiring? I had never thought my struggles could actually encourage others. Sometimes even a small comment can motivate us for months.

———

AFTER I RECOVERED FROM THE TWO SURGERIES, THE TUMOR WAS OUT OF MY body, but the harshest part of the treatment remained. To ensure no rogue cells had strayed beyond the surgical margins, I was to undergo eight intense rounds of chemotherapy. Prior to the first infusion, Dr. Braich sat down across from me in the infusion lounge chair. He asked bluntly, "Have you banked any sperm?" I shook my head and said, "Should I?"

"We're not sure how this chemotherapy regimen will affect your ability to have children. To be safe, I would advise that you bank some, but you'll need to do that in Portland."

"Well, I'm here for my first round, so let's just get started on the chemo. I don't even have a serious girlfriend, so just do your best to keep me alive, and I'll figure out the rest later." The idea of driving three hours to the city to jack off into a cup was beyond what my psyche could handle. All of this was just too much.

"Can I bring my dog in here?" I asked a nurse. I was already missing Denali. His presence alone always made me feel better. "Unfortunately, we do not allow dogs in here," she replied.

If you have not experienced an infusion room for yourself, it basically looks similar to a lounge at first glance. Leather easy chairs resembling airport massagers are lined up along walls hung with encouraging images of nature, and the nurses are friendly and warm and go from patient to patient. Look closer and you see the heaviness behind their smiles, the awareness that many patients may not respond to the promise of these noxious regimens. The nurses all wear thick, elbow-length gloves, and bags of fluid marked with hazardous waste symbols hang above the overstuffed chairs. Then you will notice the look of listless resignation and the lack of hair on some of those slumped in the chairs. Some of the patients convey a stoic optimism, recognizing the full value of each moment. Only when we are faced with parenting or our own mortality do our priorities experience such a sudden reordering.

My treatment cycle repeated every other Monday in the infusion room, where I would receive a cocktail of chemotherapy that took five hours to administer.

Watching those toxic liquids drip into my bloodstream, at each treatment, I was invariably struck by the irony. As every chemotherapy patient knows, to survive this disease, you must first endure the horrors of heavy metals and their brutal side effects. They possess an almost sadistic desire to kill the disease by first destroying the body that hosts it.

Before the final eight rounds of chemo began, a portable catheter was surgically implanted in my chest to protect my veins from the corrosive liquids. This small circular device, one inch in diameter with a rubberized center similar to a vial for an injectable liquid, was connected to a flexible tube that traveled through my veins before entering my heart. The device rested a couple of inches below my clavicle just beneath the skin, similar to a pacemaker. The nurse would punch a large-gauge needle into the port, making me feel like a test subject in a low-budget sci-fi film.

The chemotherapy drugs were then injected into tubes leading to the port, one volatile cocktail at a time, lest the toxic chemicals combine and combust. The gloved nurses would spend hours patiently injecting each brew into the circular port that protruded subcutaneously from my upper chest.

During the drive home from long days in the infusion room, neuropathy would begin in my fingertips, the numbness then slowly creeping into my hands and arms, a common side effect of the platinum-based chemo drug oxaliplatin. My sensitivity to cold was extreme, requiring me to wear gloves and scarves anytime I encountered the chilly winter air.

On a cold December evening after I had just received my second infusion, I pulled into the post office to pick up my mail on the way home. Neuropathy was already beginning to kick in as I fumbled with the key to my box. Inside was Matt Costa's self-titled first EP, which had the track "Astair" on it, a new favorite of mine. As I tried to get back inside my old Honda Civic wagon (which I had purchased in order to avoid driving my big van to the endless hospital visits), numbness was rapidly overtaking my motor function. My heart sank as I realized I had locked myself out.

Fortunately, I was adept at breaking into my own car from locking myself out so many times before. I grabbed a stick lying in the snow nearby and jammed it in my door, racing against the clock as my hands turned to unresponsive clubs. I got the door open just as I lost all sensation in my hands. The ten-minute drive home was pretty sketchy considering I could not feel the steering wheel or stick shift on my manual transmission.

The neuropathy affected my everyday routines. I could not drink tap water or any refrigerated liquid unless I warmed it up first. By day four after an infusion I would be so tired of the limitations that I would sometimes eat ice cream just to feel the frozen "burn" down my throat. My face was especially sensitive to the cold and windchill, but I would go snowboarding and cover my face as best I could. I continued to test the boundaries of what I was allowed to do, and almost pushed it too far during a Nordic ski outing with David. He waited for me at the top of a hill as I skated up, and saw something was amiss. "Are you feeling okay?" he asked. "We can head back if you're too fatigued."

"Ayyye ammm fiiiine," I slurred, my lips and cheeks feeling like I had just visited the dentist. I had left my face uncovered, and it was completely numb, pasted with snot and drool.

"We need to get you back to the lodge now!" David said with urgency. "Let's go."

Friends like David motivated me to get outside during the moments I felt like doing little else besides lying on the couch and trying my hardest to not feel sorry for myself. During several of my most miserable infusions, David would come sit with me to keep me company, one of the kindest gestures I can think of.

Years later, after I was in remission, David would take me out for breakfast and ask for advice. He had just gotten the news of a diagnosis of chronic lymphocytic leukemia. Miraculously, with the help of my oncologist Dr. Braich, David overcame the disease, and I still occasionally run into him in Bend at the climbing gym or see his converted Sprinter van on the road.

Days two, three, and four after the infusion were the worst, the chemo in my bloodstream reaching its peak of toxicity, aided by the chemo pump I wore for two days following each infusion for my secondary dose. It whirred every ten minutes, delivering another dose of poison with cruel punctuality.

Denali looked on helplessly as I fumbled to combat those nauseating and miserable days by taking antiemetic pills and vaporizing cannabis, but those seventy-two hours were a wretched existence at best. As I was left with zero energy for human interaction, Denali was the one being I could tolerate during those dark hours. In the wretched times where I found myself too sick and weak to even speak, Denali would lie at my side for hours on end, never seeming to care when I forgot to feed him his dinner until bedtime or when I would fall asleep for four hours in the middle of the day.

This is the true beauty of a great dog's love: Denali never asked anything of me, soaking up my low moments each day like a sponge that never reaches saturation, only to be ready again each time to offer love and support in return.

By the time I was halfway through my intensive rounds of chemo, Byron had begun a new relationship and felt he needed to regain his space and privacy, so I began to search for a new living situation. He had offered his place rent-free while I was there, a mutual benefit during his divorce and my diagnosis. Through a mutual friend, I'd heard that there was a little bungalow with a room available for only $150 a month. Located near the end of a dead-end street, the small house was a block from the Deschutes River and a five- or ten-minute walk from downtown Bend. Better yet, my new roommate Courtney was such a kind soul, and had an easygoing vibe that made Denali and me feel welcome.

I moved my gear into the house on a sunny and warm January day. The weathered front door was open, and reggae beats blasted pleasantly from a stereo inside. The house needed some repair, but the rent was a steal. It felt like the perfect place for Denali and me to ride out the last four months of chemo treatments. The side effects had been cumulative, growing exponentially more intense with each round. I had serious neuropathy in my hands from the oxaliplatin, especially in my fingertips. I asked Dr. Braich if there were other chemotherapy drugs that would be just as effective, concerned that I might permanently lose dexterity and feeling in my fingers. "I want to be able to climb, play guitar, and use my camera," I said. He switched me to an alternative drug, and I'm grateful typing this even now.

The new regimen did not make me lose my hair as I thought it would, and my fingers were no longer numb, but it made me vomit so violently that I was embarrassed to puke inside the house.

Courtney had cooked me a delicious and nourishing soup after a long day of infusions, but the satisfaction of the meal was short-lived. Thanking her for being so thoughtful, I sprinted out into the winter night and fell to my knees. As soon as I hit the ground, I vomited and retched until my abdominal muscles ached from turning my stomach inside out.

That same evening, I was too ill to notice when Denali chased Courtney's cat Bill up the huge ponderosa pine in the neighboring yard. The next morning, we heard him yowling from high up in the branches. I was still feeling woozy from the infusion but had no choice but to help him down. After tossing a rope over a branch twenty feet up, I climbed up hand over hand to the cat. I apologized to Bill for his night out, stuffed him in a bag, and lowered him to the ground.

Denali never did forgive that first cat that swatted him across the face when he was a puppy, or the second, the time he was getting X-rays for a broken pinkie toe.

My new next-door neighbors were a phenomenal couple, John Sterling and his wife, Heather, who used to work for Patagonia. John was the executive director of the Conservation Alliance, a collective of outdoor companies that pay annual dues to protect wild places that are under threat. Grants given to nonprofits for conservation projects now total in the millions of dollars, and it is satisfying to see the dedication of John and the Conservation Alliance to preserving the places we all enjoy for generations to come.

Back when John and I both worked from home, he would take a break and play his mandolin on their front porch, throwing pine cones at my office window while I edited photos until I would bring over my guitar and jam with him. Those jams turned into regular weekly evening sessions, and I learned to play the upright bass to balance out all the guitars. Heather would join us, singing Gillian Welch songs and accompanying me when I got to take the mic and play Greg Brown, one of my favorite songwriters. She reminded me recently that I was always wearing a huge puffy down jacket during chemo, no matter how warm it was outside.

Another side effect of chemotherapy was a hypersensitive sense of smell. This was a good thing sometimes, as I knew if I had a leak in my colostomy bag or had stepped in dog shit. But there were times it was frustrating as well.

My favorite restaurant in Bend to grab a quick bite alone was Pizza Mondo. But I had to remember to wash my hands before I arrived there. If I forgot and used their restroom, the soap reminded me of the soap in the infusion room at the hospital. I would almost puke if I washed my hands with it before I ate pizza.

After chemo, I would wander the aisles of Whole Foods, looking for anything that seemed appetizing on a delicate stomach. To stay warm, I often wore a soft and fuzzy hooded fleece jacket from Patagonia. That jacket was like a magnet, and female shoppers would pet my shoulders, offer hugs, and ask if they could feel my jacket. In the loneliness of a cancer battle, these gestures were more welcome than awkward.

During the course of my treatment I often felt like I gave off some mysterious pheromone that made me irresistible to women, even though my libido hovered at around 3 percent of normal. The combination of that and the fuzzy hoodie seemed to attract feminine attention wherever I went.

I had no mojo, and even having an erection was often painful. My first orgasm after surgery was months later and felt foreign, similar to my earliest adolescent experiences. I just "snuggled" with women that I had crushes on during that time. I was less interested in receiving pleasure or having an orgasm, but I was happy to give it. Yet I had very little emotional energy for a long-term relationship. I was focused on my survival, but welcomed affection while it was available.

I was still building up my physical stamina in other ways as well. My strength was limited, but Denali was in his prime and needed to stretch his trail legs often. Our jaunts out at Smith and in the forest service land around Bend were a welcome reprieve from the antiseptic hospital visits and helped keep my spirit from feeling too confined during my treatments. Denali's need for exercise was daily motivation to get out and breathe fresh high-desert air. His ever-intuitive friendship and the movement outdoors kept me in touch with the core of my being. It reminded me of what I was fighting for . . . why I was fighting to survive.

On one such outing, I met up with my frequent running and biking buddy Cindy to go for a trail run. Before leaving for the trails, we had made a batch of chocolate chip cookies. We came back and dropped our dogs inside while we left to grab takeout for dinner. Two full trays of cookies were on the counter, but in our hunger, we did not give them a second thought. I guess I could blame it on chemo brain as well.

When we returned, every single cookie had been consumed. Unsure whom to blame, we concluded it was most likely a team effort by both Denali and Cindy's dog, Spot. The cookies were baked with dark chocolate, toxic to dogs in higher doses, so we decided to play it safe and gave them liquids that the vet recommended to induce vomiting.

Denali was affected immediately, retching out his stomach contents into the yard for five minutes straight. I felt helpless as I watched him in his misery and empathized with his condition. "I puke ten times a day, so I feel you, bro!" I said. I then looked over at Spot, but he just stared and looked unfazed. He was too stubborn to vomit, no matter how queasy he felt. They both recovered just fine, but I learned to keep baked treats off the counter after that.

———

WESTERN MEDICINE SAVED MY LIFE, BUT ITS CHEMICALS AND STERILE CARE took a toll on my spirit. In the midst of my intense chemo regimen, my surgeon's wife recommended a local acupuncturist who had said he would be willing to see me. Each year, Keith would take on one patient's case pro bono. I was barely able to work during my treatments, so I was grateful for the support, even though I was unfamiliar with acupuncture and Chinese medicine. Keith was instrumental in my healing process, supporting my body with Eastern medicine techniques that I could feel deep in the core of my being, but could not understand. When my immune system was tapped out from the battering of chemo and radiation, his tiny needles and concoctions of Chinese herbs kept me from collapsing.

During one session, Keith mentioned ayahuasca, a psychedelic plant medicine, and said he had been studying under a shaman in Peru for years. Aloud he wondered if this same plant medicine could help me to heal and to release the years of accumulated stress and tension that could have led to my cancer in the first place.

I was entirely unfamiliar with psychedelics, only hearing horror stories about LSD frying your brain. I did a lot of research and decided to try sitting in an ayahuasca ceremony to see if it would help me. I hugged Denali in my car before going in, all the uninformed voices about the evils of psychedelics echoing in my head. I was afraid the drug would somehow change me forever.

It did change me, but the effect was quite the opposite of my fears. I learned much about myself and had profound realizations about those who had been there for me over the past year. There were hours of intense introspection, having ineffable experiences that left me feeling more grounded and even more determined to shake that black cloud of depression that still sometimes lingered.

During one ceremony, a slideshow of thirty years of my life played to me like a film in vivid detail, showing me every memory where I still held on to guilt from minor incidents in my past. Picking on my sister when I was four years old, failing to say *thank you* to my grandmother for a banana cupcake when I was only five, and on and on. Thirty years of guilt were compressed into a single hour. I spent all of the next day thinking about it, processing the weight of that revelation. How could I hold on to these petty things?

You need to let go, Ben.

To clear my head, I went free soloing at Smith Rock, climbing ropeless on easier routes until I felt centered and regrounded.

That evening in camp I sat down for another ceremony on my comfortable nest of blankets, feeling ready for what the medicine would show me next. I drank two full doses that night, more than I had dared to previously, hoping for some clarity on what I had learned the night before. I had wanted to "purge" or physically release the emotions by vomiting, but that night it simply would not happen, and I was left feeling heavy.

I had to pee, so I stepped outside into the crisp high-desert air just as the medicine began to take effect. Gazing upward, I stared at the stars shining brilliantly in the clear moonless sky, not noticing the five-inch step down to the patio. As my foot dropped to the next level, the impact jolted me from my stargazing, bringing with it the purge I had been seeking the night before. I felt a sense of relief as a projectile stream of vomit spewed out, before morphing into snakes breathing fire back at me, not wanting to come out without a fight.

"*No!*" I yelled, exhaling forcefully. I embodied the force of a dragon as I imagined breathing fire back at those snakes, consuming the shame that haunted me. I never again wanted to feel those feelings of guilt.

Later in the ceremony as I again sat quietly, I was finally able to forgive myself. When the ceremony concluded, I crawled back into my tent outside, where Denali was waiting for me. "Thank you, Denali. For sticking with me through this crazy journey, and for all those years I have been stumbling along . . . I realize I still have so much to learn." He looked at me wisely, feeling relieved to see me carrying a lighter load.

> You needed to get rid of that. I love you, friend, I'm so happy you let some of that worry go. I'm here no matter what. Okay, let's go to sleep, I've been waiting for you for hours!

I fell asleep hugging him, and slept more soundly than I had in years.

7

The Bag

I remember feeling really sad for Ben when he found
out he'd have to poop into a plastic bag, attached to his
stomach—for the rest of his life. Mainly because he
already had to put all of my poop into plastic bags.

—FROM THE SHORT FILM *DENALI*

Physically, the biggest challenge post-cancer has been my colostomy.
Wearing a colostomy bag is a major adjustment, both to self-image
and to sheer logistics. I have to make sure I carry the appropriate ostomy
supplies with me at all times, especially when traveling to remote locations. To ignore this can mean messy and embarrassing accidents. After
my surgery, I was shouldered with learning how to manage a rogue
digestive system that became uncontrollable overnight. It was an alien
experience.

Psychologically, it was even more brutal. For the first six months after the surgery, each time I finished a shower, I would pull the shower curtain to block my deformity from my own view. The sight of my altered abdomen in the large mirror that ran the length of the opposite wall was too graphic and cruel. I could barely steal a glance without my confidence wilting, and thoughts of *what woman would ever be attracted to this? How will I ever take off my shirt in public again?* overwhelming me.

Accidents were inevitable in adapting to this foreign routine, and I often felt like I had regressed to infant stage, unable to control my own bodily functions. I'd fight back tears, trying to retain my dignity as I cleaned up each foul mess. In these lowest of times, Denali would look on with a wry twinkle in his eye. You've got this, buddy—you've been dealing with my poop since I was a pup!

In public, I was often too embarrassed to expose my midriff for fear someone would see my bag, and would instead hike my jeans up higher onto my waist to hide it from view. I was able to tuck it behind my climbing harness when I climbed without a shirt, but I only really let my guard down when I was alone or with Denali. Unfazed by my insecurities, Denali never judged me. Instead, he offered support and gently leaned into me with reassurances of his devotion. It is incredible to me how a few minutes of quiet connection with him would calm my anxieties. These moments helped halt my slide into self-pity and gave me a renewed confidence to go on.

My wound care and ostomy nurse told me after my surgery that I was the first patient in thirty years of practice whom she allowed to choose the site of their stoma. I took home several colostomy bag samples and adhered them to potential stoma locations on my abdomen. I wore my climbing harness during the process, moving around the bags until I knew I found a place that it would least interfere with my active lifestyle. I settled on a placement that was low enough so my harness would not rip upward over the stoma when I fell climbing, yet high enough that it would not be too close to my intimate parts.

At the behest of that same nurse, I was visited by a fellow ostomy patient to help me adjust to my new life with the bag. He was well-meaning but three decades older and not what I would consider physically fit. I immediately felt myself tuning him out. What advice could he offer to a twenty-nine-year-old climber and surfer? How could I take seriously any advice on how to maintain an "active lifestyle" from an overweight man in his late fifties? The difference in our realities was gaping. His revolved around his golf game, and I just wanted to get back in the surf lineup and rope up for a rock climb again.

I bit my tongue and listened half-heartedly as he explained that he was still able to enjoy golfing and that he managed his digestion by "irrigating" his colon daily. I sat upright and tuned in with my full attention as he spoke of the control the irrigation process gave him in managing his handicap. "It's been life changing," he said. I did not believe his words could be true, not even a little, but to my surprise I found his advice to be the most valuable of any I received after my ordeal. It was a lesson to me to not jump to conclusions too quickly about someone, as his recommendation continues to resonate with me nearly every day in the fifteen years since.

I decided that if I could gain any semblance of routine or control, it was worth finding out more. I first asked my oncologist about irrigation, but he knew very little about it, and there was only vague information available online. I gleaned what I could and made my first attempts at giving myself a colonic through my "front butt." They were messy disasters of almost comedic proportions. Essentially, I would fill a two-liter bag that resembled a bladder from a hydration pack with body-temperature water, hanging it at shoulder level so gravity would feed the water down the tube until it reached the cone-shaped end that I gently inserted into my stoma. To allow the water to flow in, I needed to relax, breathing deeply to release all the tension in the muscles around the end of my colon. My unfamiliarity with the process made relaxation challenging; my muscles resisted, spasming every time water would enter my colon. At the time I was not aware that lying down aids in both relaxation and allowing the water to flow into the colon more freely, so I took the only advice I could find online and sat in a chair facing the toilet. A clear plastic "irrigation sleeve" was clipped onto the appliance that was adhered around my stoma, with the other end of the three-foot-long sleeve draped into the toilet bowl, cleanly guiding the poopy water where it needed to go.

The graphic visual of shit and undigested food pouring out my abdomen through a transparent sleeve was already making me feel sick, and the foul odor completely overwhelmed my overly sensitive nose. The nausea I had been battling all afternoon from my chemo infusion earlier that week violently crossed the threshold, my mouth tingling and watering. A moment later I projectile vomited, missing the toilet and spewing all over the tile floor. As I retched, the sleeve from my stoma slipped out of the toilet and released its foul contents onto the floor, adding watery chunks of feces to the vomit splattered at my feet.

The stench and sight of puke and shit on the floor only caused me to retch even more intensely, and the violence of the puking pushed me to my hands and knees. When the heaving finally paused, I sat back onto my heels and was paralyzed by shame and disgust. I was kneeling in shit, covered in puke, feeling absolutely helpless and disgusting. This was rock bottom.

I heard a knock at the door, and Byron quietly asked, "Hey, Ben, are you okay in there?" He pushed the door open, and he and Denali both stood looking concerned at the shocking sight and the dejected expression on my face.

> Dude. You look miserable. And daaaang you smell awful.
> How can I help?!?! Do you need a hug? I'm not afraid of a
> little poop.

Byron seemed unfazed by his trashed bathroom, looking at me with only compassion as he got down to business, grabbing cleaning supplies and scrubbing the floor until all evidence of my shitty accident was erased.

"I could use a hug . . . but I really need a shower," I said. "Seriously, man, I can't thank you enough."

The decision to accept the challenges of living with my colostomy quite literally saved my life as the surgery prevented my tumor from returning. Along with choosing to adopt Denali, it was one of the most important decisions of my life. Less tactful friends cracked jokes about how the bag would prevent me from making it with the ladies, and I tried not to let their insensitivity discourage me. I had my low moments and leaky mishaps during climbs, but after a few months, I came to terms with my condition and vowed that never again would I let wearing a bag hold me back. Not from intimacy, rock climbing, surfing, or anything else I dreamed of doing. I have heard countless stories of others with colostomies avoiding dating, intimacy, and the activities they love most. I hope that sharing my experience can shatter the stigma for those still afraid to live life as they did before the bag.

On a surf trip in Mexico during a break from my heavy doses of chemo, I was struggling to keep the bag adhered to my abdomen in the waves. After two hours of surfing, the salt water stripped the adhesives, and my entire kit fell off. I stuffed the useless device into the pocket of my board shorts and walked up the beach, realizing that my other ostomy supplies were an hour away in the *palapa* where I was staying. *Oh shit*, I thought, *how am I going to keep things under control on the drive back? I hope I don't crap all over myself in the car.*

My stoma protrudes nearly an inch from my abdomen, and the exposed tissues are literally mucous membranes of the inside of my colon, so they are bright red and shiny. As I walked down the beach with the end of my colon hanging out just above the top of my board shorts, a local fisherman approached. He looked at me and said, "*Hola, buen día*," and then glanced down at my belly.

His demeanor changed to one of concern, and he began freaking out, yelling and pointing at my abdomen, sure that I had been impaled. Gesturing desperately, he kept asking if I was okay. I tried to wave him off, pointing to my stoma and saying "*Cancer!*" which only caused his eyes to widen even further. I still wonder what he thought of the pasty white gringo with what looked like his guts hanging out.

Back in the rental car, I asked my friends to drive me to the nearest *farmacia*, where I bought tape, gauze, and Ziploc bags and crafted a makeshift colostomy bag out of the remedial supplies, hoping my taco lunch would not digest before we arrived back at the casa. As foul odors leaked from the breaches in the taped hack job, my friends rolled down the windows and pretended not to notice.

The summer after I completed chemo, I had gained confidence that I could manage the physical changes to my body. The emotional adjustment had been brutal, but I was eager to overcome this stigma of my handicap and fully return to my active lifestyle. Katie was in Yosemite Valley, and she invited me to come climb the Nose route on El Capitan with her. Spending a few days on the wall seemed a great way to leave behind so much of what I had faced over the past year.

I arrived in the park at midnight and stopped in a meadow to snap a couple of photos of El Capitan gloriously reflecting the light of the full moon. I had just eaten a can of smoked oysters and spilled the stinky oil all over my hands, so I jumped at every sound as I waited for the long exposures to complete, sure that every noise was a bear. When I arrived at camp, I realized there were already the maximum number of climbers in the campsite we were sharing, so I camped in the back of Katie's tiny Ford Focus hatchback. At some Yosemite campgrounds, it is prohibited to sleep in cars, especially in the historic Camp 4, where park rangers patrol regularly and use thermal cameras to seek out offenders. As I was peeking out of the curtain she had put up to obscure a view of the little sleeping quarters she had made, unassuming rangers wandered by, not even considering the little two-door hatchback as a place to search for sleeping dirtbags.

At that point, I was still unaware of the low testosterone levels caused by my radiation treatments or chemo, or both. This less than adequate supply of the male hormone resulted in a weakened state and a lack of motivation. The meager reserves of energy that remained were simply not up to the task, and by the end of our first day on the wall, I was utterly taxed from climbing and from managing the hundred-pound haul bags that held all of our food and camping gear. After eating a cold dinner from cans, we made camp on the wall. Katie took the top bunk, hanging her portable sleeping ledge from anchor bolts in the wall, suspended a few feet above the narrow granite shelf where I would sleep that night. We wore our climbing harnesses while we slept. I made sure I was tied in close to the wall so I would not roll off the three-foot-wide ledge. It was hard to sleep, as the shelf sloped at an angle before dropping to the valley floor five hundred feet below. I would begin to roll over the edge, stopping suddenly when my harness caught and jolted me awake to a view of the empty abyss below.

I was awakened at two a.m. by the uncomfortable sensation of my stomach gurgling, my colostomy bag filling to the point of nearly bursting. *Oh, please no, not now!* I thought, sitting up in my sleeping bag, careful not to roll onto the taut shit receptacle protruding from my abdomen. If the contents of the colostomy bag exploded, my sleeping bag and only set of clothes would be unbearable.

As I carefully changed my full poop bag by headlamp, I hoped the disgusting smell would not wake up Katie, sleeping only a few inches away. Wearing a harness complicated the process, and my stomach showed no sign of settling down. I had missed two days of my "flush," and my digestion had become an unruly mess up there. After I finished, I was emotionally thrashed but stunned by the beauty of the crisp night sky. I sat there for an hour, lost in the magic of the Milky Way and the moonlight reflecting off Middle Cathedral, the large formation across the meadow. In spite of my handicaps, survivor's guilt, and PTSD from the cancer experience, sitting there among the majesty of those granite walls made me grateful to be alive.

As time passed, I became more comfortable with navigating the inconvenience and daily routine of my colostomy. In the fall of 2006, I was hired for a six-day photo shoot in Joshua Tree National Park, California, with a new outdoor fashion brand called Nau. My dear friend Eugénie, the art director for Nau, hired a crew of our creative friends to come along and model for the shoot. We had a great time camping amid the granite domes where Denali and I had spent so many of our early experiences together. Over the next few days, I ate way too many energy bars and too much trail mix, and the combination wreaked havoc on my digestive system. I farted constantly, and even though the smell was diffused by the charcoal filters in the colostomy bags, the awkwardness of my ostomy interrupted the most peaceful moments. This often happened just as I leaned in close to a model, composing an image backdropped by the serenity of a granite dome and the sunset vista of Joshua trees.

"Oh, be quiet!" I would exclaim, attempting to overcome my embarrassment.

"Earrrrrrrrl, why do you have to be so loud," Eugénie joked.

"Earl. Seems appropriate for his inappropriate nature . . . that's gotta be his name from now on," I said, laughing out loud. And thus, my uncontrollable, belly-farting little front-butt gremlin found his name.

A few years later I found myself backstage after a Michael Franti and Spearhead show. A band member had invited my girlfriend at the time and her sister to hang out there. My mind was elsewhere as the conversations failed to go beyond superficial small talk. Bored, I searched for an excuse to leave early. I scratched my belly, involuntarily lifting my shirt in the process. The bass player saw my exposed colostomy bag and said, "Dude what's up with your stomach? You all good?"

I shared briefly that I had survived colon cancer and that it was simply my colostomy bag. There was a drastic shift in mood as things suddenly got real. The conversations that followed held much more substance. Since then I have often caught myself subconsciously exposing my bag, using my handicap as a means to connect.

The disasters involving Earl became far less frequent, but I still had my share of embarrassing moments. I decided to join my girlfriend and her sister to go see a few friends play the Sasquatch! Music Festival, a four-and-a-half-hour drive from Portland. We packed to camp overnight, but we ended up bickering all day long, so we decided to leave early, driving late into the night without grabbing dinner.

The hungrier we became, the sillier the arguments grew until out of desperation we made a stop at Burger King, the only establishment serving food at three a.m. This was my first fast food in over a decade, but I thought, *What the hell, it can't be that bad.*

I was so very wrong.

That evening, the bickering continued as we arrived back in Portland and my girlfriend popped an Ambien. "Hey," I said, "no fair, I'll take one too—actually, I only want half," resigning myself to the fact that I probably just needed to end this day with all its petty arguing and start fresh the next morning.

The sun woke me, and as I fought to open my drugged eyelids, I felt an odd sensation surrounding Earl, as if he were pressurized. Too groggy to register what was happening, I rolled onto my stomach and buried my face in the pillow in a vain attempt to prolong my sleep. I felt a sense of relief in the pressure around my stoma, and then a horrible odor slapped me wide awake.

"Oh no!" I groaned, waking my partner up.

"Gross! What's that smell?!" she exclaimed.

"I think I pooped the bed. I'm never eating Burger King again. Or taking Ambien, for that matter."

I leaped up, stripped the shit-stained sheets, and sprinted for the shower.

Lesson learned, I thought. *I fed you shit, so you made me shit. Earl, you certainly know how to keep life interesting.*

Living with a colostomy has taught me volumes over the years about awareness and patience, and, most importantly, how to simply slow down. Never once have I felt rejected by a friend or a woman I am interested in when I share that I have a bag. Most times, I felt like it helped strip away the pretenses and move things into an authentic space.

Earl has helped me be more conscious about what I put into my body, especially with hydration. In order to irrigate and clear out my system for the day, I must be fully hydrated, or my bowels will stubbornly refuse to do anything. If I am dehydrated, my colon will simply absorb the water instead of stimulating them to move.

If I choose to ignore my fullness during a meal and partake in a second portion or dessert, my system will override my daily colonic, sending my stomach and stoma into spasms as my bowels attempt to push shit through the pinkie-finger-sized hole of my stoma.

The threat of this discomfort helps me to resist unhealthy impulses. Too much alcohol, and I'm dehydrated. Too much processed food or sugar, and I become gassy as hell. In turn I have become more conscious of how foods will affect my moods and energy levels. I need protein, especially eggs early in the morning. I need a steady stream of healthy snacks, but I prefer not to eat big sit-down meals.

I have also become more cognizant of my body image, both in how I perceive myself and how others perceive me. If I am stressed, the tension will inhibit things from moving during a flush. When I am camping, hearing a line forming outside the pit toilet I am using to flush will cause me to tense up, slowing down the process and only further frustrating those waiting. It has taught me to let go of others' opinions and my own stress, realizing that I cannot will my body to do anything faster than it wants to.

With the bag comes humility, as I am forced to accept my limitations. My body is changed permanently, and I am always at risk of a hernia. I have a visible handicap in tropical climates and surf breaks when I am wearing board shorts, or in intimate moments. The vulnerability shifts from visible to audible when I fart uncontrollably during a silent yoga class or meditation. Or when I reach to shake hands during an important business meeting. Or while filming a musician in the recording studio during the perfect vocal take.

Earl has helped me to slow down. The twenty or thirty minutes I need to flush is now my quiet time, a routine I have grown to appreciate. Because it takes another half an hour to quiet my stomach after a flush, it means that on photo or film shoots I must get up an hour earlier than the crew. This can mean a three or four a.m. alarm. Other times I need to stay up hours later while everyone else is sleeping peacefully.

I have done my flush while covered in ravenous mosquitoes on a small island in Lake Superior, sitting on a log in the Mexico jungle—where I was also easy prey for hungry, winged insects—or inside a freezing cold pit toilet after a long day of climbing, or a smelly and hot porta-potty while baking in the high noon sunshine.

Accidents still happen when I am careless, reminding me to be present and aware of my actions. Nothing is more humbling than having to clean up my own poop off a friend's floor and having to wash my clothes after I sprayed them with shit.

A couple of years ago, I lost yet another friend to colon cancer, and I knew I needed to be more open about my own battle. With trepidation, I decided to post a shirtless photo of myself with my colostomy bag fully visible. This was the first time I had ever publicly shared an image with my bag exposed, and I was showing it to over a hundred thousand people. I wrote this caption, fingers trembling as I hit send on the post:

I've had a colostomy since 2004, after being diagnosed at age 29 with colorectal cancer, but it took 13 years to finally for the first time share an image of all of me, with my colostomy bag fully visible.

It's funny how ego, self-image and fear can make such a difficult obstacle of a surgery that quite literally saved my life. My ostomy nurses let me choose the site, so I had the doctors place my ostomy below the belt of my climbing harness to avoid injury. Because my stoma is below the belt line, I could often hide that I wore "a bag."

The chemo and radiation were brutal, but adjusting to having a "front butt" was a huge emotional challenge . . . I couldn't bear to see myself naked in the mirror for months, and getting my digestion dialed was a long and painful process.

Thankfully, someone introduced me to daily irrigation technique—essentially a colonic—to gain control over it all, and most days I wear a small stoma cap instead of a large bag and am often able to forget about it.

Educate yourself on the symptoms of colorectal cancer and insist on a colonoscopy if you suspect something—I would not be here today if my nurse practitioner had not recommended that I have one. I've lost two friends under the age of 35 to the disease this year and have other younger comrades who are still battling this insidious disease. Age is irrelevant for colon cancer, do not let the info out there about "it's an over 60 disease" lull you into a false comfort as it almost did me.

I've been using ostomy products by a small company called Cymed for the past 14 years. Created by a swimmer, they are the only ostomy appliances that stay secure when I surf, swim, rock climb or practice yoga. If you're an ostomate, look their products up. They have drastically improved my quality of life. If you have a colostomy, definitely look into irrigation—it's challenging at first, but it's truly a game changer.

ben_moon

22,786 likes

MARCH 21, 2018

My fears were ungrounded. That post was by magnitudes the most-engaged-with and commented-on post I had ever publicly made, receiving nearly 23,000 likes and over 1,600 comments. I received several direct messages over the next few weeks, with people sharing that they or their loved ones had symptoms and that my post had helped them have the courage to see their physician. A few friends also got checked out and their colonoscopies revealed precancerous polyps, the removal of which most likely saved their lives. That overwhelming response convinced me that sharing my story on these pages was more important than my desire to remain private about my life.

A colostomy is a shitty burden to live with, but I would not change a thing. If Earl is happy, I'm happy. If he's grumpy, watch out.

8

Return to Life

"Your cancer is in remission." When I first heard those words, they seemed miraculous, but as in summiting a high alpine peak, the battle is only halfway resolved. You must descend the mountain safely before you can return to your "normal" life. I quickly realized that the new normal bore little resemblance to my selfish perspectives and priorities prior to cancer.

Toxic chemicals remained in my bloodstream and tissues for years, creating adolescent mood swings and causing my sweat to reek of chemicals and heavy metals. Radiation and chemo slowed my testosterone production, causing fatigue, depression, and muscle weakness.

Once friends heard the good news of my remission, the constant flow of love and energetic support they had shown me during treatment stopped. They certainly never meant to hurt me, but I'm a sensitive man, and the sudden feeling of abandonment plunged me into dense and disorienting darkness. One's struggle with cancer does not end the moment the body's normal cells take over. The scars take years to heal.

During the peak of the battle, from the confusion of diagnosis to the debilitating treatments that follow, life is lived in a uniquely present state. I felt fully engaged in each moment because I had no option to do otherwise. No long-term plans could be made, so the only choice was to endure what each hour might bring, often waiting for a doctor to call with the latest prognosis or a new treatment protocol.

In many ways, dealing with cancer is a gift, enabling us to live as a dog sees the world. Denali never seemed to live in the future or the past. Instead he simply responded to the joy and struggle and stimulus that resides in the here and now. When the storms of life swirled, Denali would often breathe a huge sigh, letting go of any weight as he relaxed into the present moment.

On April 13, a week before my thirtieth birthday, the final toxic chemotherapy cocktail was administered into my bloodstream. My body was overloaded with chemicals and out of whack, but the emotional relief I felt overcame all the physical discomfort. Never again would I sit and endure those poisons being pumped into my veins. Now my goal was to purge what toxicity remained and regain my strength and fitness. "Denali! Let's gooooooo, buddy. Thank you so much for sticking by me through all this." He licked my cheek, and then we sat quietly. I leaned in, and he did the same until our foreheads touched. We supported one another's weight there for a long, long time, exchanging love and gratitude. I was so incredibly grateful for this dog. My friend. And to be alive to share more time and adventures outside together.

A week later, I awoke to the first day of my thirties. I felt a monumental shift, as if I was beginning a new life. The prospect of not needing to be in that leather infusion room chair relieved me. Never again would I inhale those horrible chemical smells and sanitizing soaps with their awful clinical fragrance.

To me, birthdays are a personal affair. No one else should be responsible for making that day special. It's up to you to do that. This day, I wanted to spoil myself like I never had before. I awoke before sunrise and gave Denali a huge hug. My first stop was to practice yoga at my favorite studio in downtown Bend, celebrating afterward with a solo meal at my favorite local breakfast spot followed by a deep-tissue massage.

Blissed out from a pleasant morning taken at my own pace, I took Denali to meet up with a good friend, and we hiked to the back side of Smith Rock, our goal a popular multi-pitch route up the Monkey Face formation.

Monkey Face is a 350-foot spire that is the centerpiece of Smith Rock State Park. When viewed from the south, the top of the pillar resembles the face of a monkey complete with a mouth, nose, and eyes. The view from the summit is breathtaking—a beautiful line of the Cascade giants stretches from north to south and includes Mount Hood, Mount Jefferson, Three Fingered Jack, Mount Washington, North Sister, Middle Sister, South Sister, Broken Top, and Mount Bachelor.

We topped out our climb at sunset and sat there for a long while. I reflected on what it meant for me to turn thirty and have a new chance at living. It felt like so much possibility lay ahead of me, and I drank in the feeling of life. "No more treatments!" I exclaimed, almost afraid to say it out loud.

There is an airy free-hanging rappel from the summit of the formation, an exposed two hundred feet to the ground. As I lowered myself and the rope slid smoothly through my belay device, the yellow rays of last light streamed through the notch where the Monkey connects to the main wall. The soft light felt like a symbol of closure for the chapter I was leaving behind.

Denali was there to greet me at the base. I held him extra close. "We're going to get through this, my friend."

Yes. Yes, we are! You never leave me again, okay?!
No more scares.

A full moon was lighting up the volcanic walls as we scrambled over Asterisk Pass, a sketchy shortcut to the front side, the most popular area to climb within the park. As we walked along the base of the wall, I saw that Chain Reaction, my favorite climb in the area, was lit up theatrically.

I asked my climbing partner, "Would you mind giving me a catch on Chain? I think it's bright enough out to climb it . . . It's been an incredible day, and it would be the perfect ending if I can send this line cleanly in only the moonlight."

I roped up and tentatively climbed the fifteen feet to the first bolt. Feeling more confident, I let muscle memory and intuition take over, carefully placing my feet in the faint light of the moon. When I reached the anchors, I was elated. Sitting back and leaning into the rope, I took a deep breath and absorbed the love I felt from the moon, from the day, from life, from simply everything. *I'm going to get through this. I refuse to just survive; I must live my life fully now.*

With the worst behind me, I celebrated my return to life by climbing every chance I had. Denali was ecstatic to be back in our old routine, living life on our terms instead of on a chemo schedule. I celebrated with my local climbing community, laughing and sharing belays as we took turns climbing laps on a few of my favorite lines. When the celebrations subsided, I felt a little frightened. The prospect of a future beyond just the next day or week was overwhelming. I had been living day to day for nearly a year. *Dare I make any plans?* I worried. *What if the tumor comes back? What if no woman will ever love me now that I'm "well"? Will they all be turned off by my poop bag? Am I too scarred to be able to care for a partner, or am I too self-absorbed after a year of focusing on my battle?*

> Dude. Stop worrying so much! You have me,
> let's just go on a road trip! We'll figure this out.

Denali always had his priorities straight.

———

TWO WEEKS AFTER MY LAST ROUND OF CHEMOTHERAPY, DR. AZIN REMOVED my chemo port through the same scar where he had inserted it six months prior. The region had become so scarred that it required a tug-of-war between Dr. Azin and the scar tissue. Under the local anesthetic I could only feel the tension as he pulled out the port, but the sound of tearing tissues was disconcerting. It was as if my body did not want to let go of this last physical reminder of the illness and treatments that had become my very identity over the past year.

As I started feeling better, I recognized that I was now physically able to start booking photography gigs. Emotionally, I had not yet fully recovered. Making long-term plans was something I had not considered for over a year, and the continual challenges of finding photography work as a freelancer and dealing with the day-to-day routine of life was daunting.

Life after cancer: Everyone thinks that should be joyous and a reason to celebrate, which it is. But others cannot know the hell you have just endured. I haven't returned from war, or been freed from prison, but I imagine there are some similarities to the frightening and scary world that awaits you after a prolonged battle with cancer. Suddenly, you are faced with seemingly limitless possibilities of choice after a year within the confines and safety of a regimented schedule. It can be terrifying, all that choice in a world where no one really understands what you've been through.

"Get over it, you survived, you're here now. You should stop talking about cancer so much."

The words stung, especially considering they came from my new girlfriend. I felt confused and misunderstood, devastated by her insensitivity.

How could I explain to her that I was forever changed, that no matter how much I wanted to, I could never go back? Despite the horrors of cancer, I recognized that I had little desire to return to the years before the diagnosis. The insights I had involuntarily gained through this ordeal were far too precious to move beyond.

On a recent film project that documented the journey of cancer survivors and patients, I met an oncology nurse who was in her last rounds of chemo for colorectal cancer. She shared that during her battle with cancer, she sometimes felt that she was labeled with a *C* stamp and was misunderstood. I could relate to that. As soon as the news was out that I had cancer, it seemed that people simply did not know how to treat me. There were the pitying stares, the averted glances, and the awkward comments. My friends felt sorry for me yet often did not know how to act around or relate to me. I knew they could not help but feel that my disease was a death sentence.

There were even those who commented in the most insensitive ways, but I was fighting for my life and it was a waste of my precious energy to allow their carelessness about my feelings to bother me.

I was ghosted by some, observing that they steered clear of interactions with me. I was not offended, aware that my diagnosis brought them face-to-face with their mortality, possibly for the first time. It was the ultimate relationship distiller, and those still standing after the refining process stuck by me through it all, reaching out during the low moments, dropping off home-cooked meals, and even sitting with me in the infusion room during chemo treatments.

I felt very similarly about divorce, especially growing up around a stigma that it meant somehow you had failed or not tried hard enough. The *D* stamp felt especially shameful among those I had gone to Bible meetings with. When I finally filed for divorce and cleaned up all the life details that came with it, I felt immense guilt for ending the marriage even though Melanie had moved away and made it clear she preferred no contact with me.

The only steady and trustworthy confidant through it all was Denali. He did not look at me with pitying eyes or just tell me to "get over it." Instead Denali leaned in, steadied me, and helped me get up and move when all I wanted to do was stay in bed and never talk to anyone again.

———

DURING MY CHEMOTHERAPY TREATMENTS, I WAS STILL TAKING ZOLOFT FOR depression, but I was popping so many pills amid the doctor visits and laps to the hospital and infusion room that I kept forgetting to take my Zoloft. I was almost out of my last refill and felt so full of chemicals that I decided just to come off it cold turkey. I figured that the change would not even faze me, but it was a wild ride. For four years my serotonin levels had been artificially manipulated, and now my brain struggled to regain its balance. Add the residual heavy metals from the chemo and the fact that I had been numbed to my full emotional capacity for four years, without Zoloft to temper my feelings, I now felt every emotion like a raw nerve ending. I felt like a teenager again.

Happy. Sad. Really Happy. Happy. Really sad. I was on a roller coaster.

But I made it through, and I have not taken another antidepressant since that day.

Since then, I have come to fully understand how seasonal affective disorder influences me. I need trips to the tropics and sunshine during the darkest weeks of winter. If I cannot travel, I use every tool at my disposal to make those months brighter. Lots of surfing, and if there are no waves, I swim laps in the local pool. When it is dark in the morning, I use light therapy to help me wake up and stay energized. I have vaped high-CBD cannabis flower, and even utilized subperceptual microdoses of psychedelics for their antidepressant and antianxiety effects.

I also now recognize how toxic and isolating the maelstrom of stress and anxiety disorders can be. One of my surgical specialists brushed me off when I shared my theory that the malignant tumor in my rectum was caused by stress and from the internalization of pain I felt amid the feelings of betrayal and failure. At the time of my divorce, I was only twenty-five years old and lacked a true community and supportive friendships. I had no release, nowhere to safely let go of these feelings.

I have since sought to eliminate negative relationships from my life and have little patience for those that continually drag me down. I gravitate toward those who live with gratitude and positivity and avoid downers and narcissists like the plague. This is not just to make life more pleasant, it is for my health, my survival, and my very existence. Cling to the positive and let go of the negative. Your life depends on it.

Cancer also shifted my perspectives on achievement and pinnacle moments of achievement. My early career desire was to photograph athletes at the height of their progression, ascending the hardest rock climbing route or surfing the gnarliest wave. This fascination with athletic prowess transformed into insatiable curiosity for human emotion and all of its manifestations. I began to seek out more meaningful relationships and discover human stories with greater depth to document, observing and learning about human connection and emotion.

This has resulted in a drastic shift in my work from before to after cancer. I shared this observation in a talk I gave at my hospital to cancer families, patients, and survivors. I asked the audience if they could see a visual shift in my work from before cancer to after. They all agreed that a palpable shift had occurred in my work, to a deeper sensitivity and awareness of those I photographed.

Surviving cancer also made me realize how interconnected we are with one another and recognize the importance of true friendship. After going through that battle, I have shifted my focus to relationships and having adventures with those I care about. In my own athletic endeavors, I still contemplate risk. I am aware that to feel truly alive I must push myself outside my comfort zone, by committing to make the drop down a seemingly impossible steep wave face, or to find the flow state while tiptoeing through the no-fall zone on a climb.

This quest to further understand and document human emotion has helped me overcome my shyness and fear of portraiture. For a decade I avoided eye contact with my subjects in my images, using more of a fly-on-the-wall approach. My excuse was that Patagonia preferred candid imagery, so I worked hard to document moments without interfering with the vibe of the scene. I realize this was also an excuse, one that further reinforced my shyness. Shooting portraits was terrifying because it meant I needed to engage with others.

For the past twelve years, I have been shooting portraits for a series I simply call *Faces*. I moved back to Portland a few years after my treatment ended, invigorated by the creative energy I found there. I lived in the northwest corner of the city, just steps from the five-thousand-acre Forest Park. Every afternoon, the white wall of the three-story building next door bounced perfect reflected light into my kitchen.

Inspired by a Mark Seliger portrait series shot in natural light in his studio's stairwell, I began shooting tight portraits of my friends and of creatives that I collaborated with. All of my early portraits were shot in the same location, but I eventually realized I could find that same quality of light nearly anywhere during the daylight hours, and I later converted the portraits into black-and-white images to keep the series aesthetically uniform. The location, clothing, and colors in the portraits are irrelevant; they are only about sharing the essence of the individual. The *Faces* project allows me to capture a meaningful portrait of anyone, anywhere in the world, without the need for planning or setup or props.

This has been an ongoing personal project—one that I have found to be the most enriching photo series I have ever worked on. Shooting these portraits has offered a means to deeply connect with and honor the inspiring individuals I have encountered along this journey. Seeing others drop their guard and share their true selves with me in my portraiture has enabled me to heal from my years of shyness and intense fear of being open and vulnerable with my own story.

Whenever I would hear Denali sigh, it seemed as if he was fully releasing every ounce of stress he had encountered in his day. I often ask the subjects of my portraits to close their eyes and take a deep breath before letting it all out in one huge sigh. This pause enables my subjects to open up and show their true selves, allowing me a rare glimpse into their souls, the distillation of their essence without false smiles or any other superfluous fronts. In Denali's sigh was a reminder not to take life too seriously, and this same momentary suspension of insecurity helps me to capture a person's true essence on camera.

In the physiological sense, a sigh is a simple exhalation of breath, but it is so much more than just that. It is truly letting go, settling into a deeper acceptance of the present moment. When dogs sigh, they offer a warm embrace of contentment to those near enough to receive.

9

Connections

Karass: A group of people linked in a cosmically sig-
nificant manner, even when superficial linkages are
not evident

We're all connected.

As Denali and I traveled the West prior to my diagnosis, I
lived the lifestyle of a vagabond climber and outdoor adventure photographer with a wise and adventure-seasoned sidekick always at my
side. With Denali's gift of winning the hearts of strangers, together
we forged new connections, expanding our community of like-minded
travelers and creatives. Many of those connections have resulted in
lifelong friends and frequent collaborators on my creative endeavors.

During my cancer treatments, I received immense support from
this community, but because I rarely had energy to socialize face-to-
face in the days following chemo infusions, Denali was my pillar. He
stood by me throughout the entirety of the journey, propping me up

with steady support I desperately needed but could not ask for from another human. Never weary of giving, Denali offered his love freely, never asking anything in return.

> What do you need, Ben? I just want to help. How can I get those yucky feelings to stop?!
>
> Sheesh . . . you just puked again!!
>
> Last time I puked that much was when I ate that rotten sandwich in the van. Oops, I didn't mean to admit that.
>
> Here, what if I lick your hand and lean into you . . . Is this okay? Because I'll come even closer . . . I'm here for you, here's another face lick just to be sure you know that.

Denali was my closest friend, the one I leaned into in those bleak moments when the hopeless void of malaise and nausea seemed too great to overcome. Yet once I was given the green light from doctors that my cancer was in remission, I had to relearn how to live. I had to relearn my place within social circles, hustle to win back old photography clients, and find new climbing partners. Denali was my through line, the one constant within the confusion. His enthusiasm for being outside helped me to regain my stamina, and during our adventures close to home I started shooting photos that I felt good about. The better I felt physically and creatively, the stronger my images and other friendships became.

Denali also exhibited two distinct personality traits that closely mirrored my own inner conflicts. One was his loving and cuddly side with a need for closeness and connection, and the other was an indomitable independent streak that he exercised often: the need to wander and feel free. I assumed that the urge to roam came from his husky and wild canid origins, and the loyal and needy qualities from his pit bull terrier pedigree.

I had a tendency to draw out romantic relationships far beyond their expiration date, feeling a sense of allegiance to the time I had invested with my partner, but inevitably my self-preservation instincts would kick in, and I would break free and spend the next six months to a year on a solo journey of independence before settling down once again.

A year after treatment, I was starting to feel more like myself and was finally making images I felt were worthy of submitting to Patagonia. I was in the thick of an immense photo edit for a submission that was past deadline, and I knew that Denali needed to get in a good run or mountain bike ride. I wanted to wrap up since the job had taken me all week to complete, so I attempted to buy an hour or two and gave Denali a rawhide bone to chew on. I knew that this would appease his restlessness and keep him content for a while. I returned to my home office, intent on finishing the color correction on the five hundred or so images I submitted to Jane Sievert every three or four months.

When I finally emerged from my image-editing cave, I realized that it had been oddly quiet for longer than usual. Denali had not yet asked to come in, but I was sure he was happy with his bone. At that moment, the phone rang and a representative from Newport Avenue Market, an upscale grocer a couple of miles to the west, asked, "Are you missing a dog? Because a dog named Denali with this number on his tag was found wandering the food aisles and has been barking and hanging out with our customers."

I had walked and biked to the market several times, and each time Denali seemed miffed as I tied his leash near the entrance. I was mortified that he had crossed two busy streets in route to this Shangri-la of delectable smells but had to chuckle as I pictured him sitting outside the automatic sliding doors until they opened and then pleading with shoppers to share the spoils that were heaped in their carts with him.

I asked at customer service where I could find him, and they laughed and said he was in the office upstairs. Opening the door to the room, I found him on his back in a state of utter bliss, circled by store employees who were giving him ear scratches and belly rubs. He looked perturbed that I had come for him so soon and cut short his fun.

How could I be mad at him? Denali had been so patient through my treatments and recovery, and now he was as restless as I felt. We were both ready to roam free again.

Denali was a masterful escape artist, as adept at ghosting from any scenario as I was with leaving awkward social events. He often would disappear, doing his well-practiced Irish goodbye the moment I was feeling relieved to finally be all packed and ready to leave for a road trip.

His wandering ways continued throughout the years of his prime, and especially during our last few years in Bend after my cancer treatments had wrapped up. Denali loved adventure but never quite made peace with traveling by vehicle, so whenever he would see me loading the bags into our Honda Element, he lazed nearby in the sunshine until I turned my back.

One such occurrence happened the morning of a photo shoot for Ruffwear, a canine adventure gear brand I often shot images for. Denali was scheduled to model their backpacks and safety harnesses that day. I threw my camera bag in and closed the door of my rig to leave. I glanced back to Denali's bed and saw he had slipped out quietly.

I was distraught that I had to leave for the shoot without knowing where he was, but since the shoot was nearby and I knew he would show up soon, I asked my neighbor Heather to keep her eye out for him. Sure enough, thirty minutes later Heather called, letting me know that Denali had returned and was safe at my house. I joked to the creative director that Mr. Redford was now in the makeup trailer getting freshened up and would be ready after a nap and a light lunch.

Distinguished and handsome even into his later years, Denali had been nicknamed Robert Redford and Paul Newman, especially while on Ruffwear photo shoots. He appeared in the company's catalogs for over a decade, earning the title of their "longest running model," even surpassing the number of appearances by the dogs of Ruffwear founder Patrick Kruse.

I dreamed of the day I could attach a GPS to Denali's collar and save myself hours of searching and worry. Eventually, through studying his patterns and getting tips from my neighbors and friends, I became savvy to the rhythms of his explorations and urban adventures. He would typically slip down the dirt path to the Deschutes River and then wander up the hill, eating food left in the neighbor dogs' and cats' bowls before working his way to the top of Awbrey Butte, sometimes ending up at the house owned by the Sherpa family. This happened so often that I had their number programmed into my cell phone.

In one occurrence, one of the Sherpa kids called to tell me that Denali was again at their house, and I arrived in the dark, pausing as I saw the scene projected clearly through the window.

Denali sat wagging his tail in the kitchen, surrounded by adults who were doting on him. I knocked, then slipped in quietly and stood there until he saw me.

Denali dropped to the floor with a mixture of shame and astonishment, realizing that he was caught red-handed for the first time. "He's so cute! We've been feeding him steak," someone said. "No wonder you wandered up there every chance you got!" I exclaimed as we biked back home. His misbehavior was rarely mischievous, rather an almost subconscious result of his insatiable northern dog appetite and instinct to feast, as well as Denali's lifelong ambition of expanding his and my ever-growing circle of human friends.

Similar to Denali's knack for dropping into interactions that would evolve into lifelong friendships, both my entire photography career and lifestyle have been built organically through chance meetings and opportune happenstance, and simply being drawn to those who shared similar, often indescribable motivations. Those friendships in the outdoor and music communities after I survived cancer and the interconnectedness of these tribes reveal themselves often, even to this day.

When I was working at Metolius back in 2001, a co-worker and fellow surfer named Ron House had played me a handful of bootleg tunes from an up-and-coming surf filmmaker named Jack Johnson. At the time, long before he became famous, Jack was simply making surf movies and writing music while traveling on surf trips with his friends. During my core "dirtbag" years wandering in the van with Denali, the soundtrack for his first movie, a sixteen-millimeter surf film called *Thicker Than Water* that he made with Chris Malloy, provided inspiration during the long drives and cold winter nights on the road. At the time, I was unaware of how much Jack's music would have an impact on my life and career following my battle with cancer.

While I was recovering from treatments, Jack would play the

outdoor amphitheater each summer in Bend. What caught my ear at a few early shows were his covers of my favorite Greg Brown songs, "Sleeper" and "Spring Wind," often falling on unappreciative ears. I wanted to sing along at the top of my lungs.

Music had meant so much to me throughout my healing process, both in recovering from the divorce that altered my life's trajectory and the cancer that nearly killed me. Music was the only thing besides Denali that I felt I could turn to. It was my trusted confidant, a place to open my most vulnerable musings and private inner dialogue. I found everything else to be too exhausting. Music and Denali. Neither asked questions, and both were there to nourish and lift me up whenever I needed them. I would simply snuggle with Denali, listening to the music that made me feel whole again.

During my intense chemo treatments, Sonnie—my old climbing buddy—offered to introduce me to Gerry Lopez, whom he had met through his role as brand ambassador for Patagonia. Gerry is a legendary figure in the surfing world from his days of mastering the Pipeline, a reef break on the North Shore of Oahu. Gerry had settled in Bend, so we swung by his surfboard-shaping shop. I was nervous to meet such a legendary figure, but Gerry's calm demeanor put me immediately at ease. As he extended his hand to shake mine, Earl let out a loud fart before I realized it was happening. I was horrified, but Gerry just smiled kindly and shared, "It's all good, bro, I used to have one of those too." He lifted his shirt to show me the scar on his abdomen. "I fell on my fin surfing years ago and sliced my colon. The doctors gave me a colostomy for six months while it all healed up."

A few weeks later, Gerry invited me to come surf the "ditch wave" the day of a Jack Johnson show. Jack was there too. The Ditch was a standing wave located in, of all places, an unassuming irrigation canal that wound through the monochrome high-desert landscape. Formed by the constriction of the walls of the canal combined with a drop in elevation, the wave was stationary and predictable, providing a place for surfers to ride their boards far from the ocean. It was a bizarre scene: a line of five to ten surfers waiting their turn for the wave, the smell of juniper and sage blending pleasantly with the nostalgic aroma of sunscreen and surf wax.

Jack carved back and forth on a small five-foot four-inch surfboard Gerry had shaped for this A-frame-shaped peak of rushing water, and Denali walked down the concrete-lined embankment and began to bark at him, trying to convince Jack that what he was doing was unsafe, but his warnings fell on unreceptive ears.

Jack, come back to shore!

Ben, you too. Why did you go to the other side?

I hollered at Denali that Jack was fine and to please leave him alone, snapping a few images of him surfing from the opposite bank. Denali looked at me, then at Jack, shook his head, and resumed his attempts to coax Jack out of the irrigation canal wave and onto solid ground.

Can you not hear me? I'll try to speak louder . . .

Why aren't you listening?

The current is so fast, and that little floaty thing you're flinging around doesn't look safe.

Oh, you're coming out?! Finally. I was getting worried you couldn't hear. I'll lean into you a little.

That evening, Jack and his wife Kim offered me an all-access pass and let me photograph the show. It was exhilarating to snap photos in the pit at the front edge of the stage as Jack played to eight thousand fans. When he covered "Spring Wind," I sat down and closed my eyes to enjoy the moment. After the show I thanked him for playing the song and for giving me the opportunity to shoot. Kim offered me an ice cream cone and showed me around backstage as we chatted about our mutual acquaintances in the conservation world.

In the years since, Jack and Kim have continued to inspire me, both with their conservation efforts with All At Once—eliminating single-use plastics from their tour, encouraging the use of refillable water bottles, raising awareness of plastic pollution in the oceans, and supporting education through the Kōkua Hawai'i Foundation—and repeatedly elevating the visibility of up-and-coming musicians such as Matt Costa and, more recently, my friend John Craigie by giving them an opportunity to perform in front of larger audiences. Through the life they lead, Jack and Kim have shown the power of community and how elevating the exposure of other artists brings positivity to the world. Jack's example of doing what you love, being a good person, staying true to who you are, giving back, and lifting up other artists has been a source of inspiration in my own creative journey. Taking just a few minutes to connect and offer kindness can shift someone's future.

While photographing Jack performing for eight thousand fans, I felt a creative energy flow through me that I had never experienced. My love for music merged with my eye for capturing moments, and I felt utterly alive. I never dreamed that this opportunity to shoot a show would lead to so many others to photograph, collaborate with, and film musicians. Many of those same artists are now some of my closest friends.

At first, my connection to the music world was just photographing live shows with Jack Johnson and Matt Costa, but since then, I have made photographs for albums and press kits for Blind Pilot, Modest Mouse, Jack Johnson, Brett Dennen, Menomena, Guster, John Craigie, the Shook Twins, and many others. Feeling that synergy of working with another artist, especially someone who creates music, is an experience that is fulfilling on the deepest of soul levels.

Collaborating with the musicians and artists who had meant so much to me through those times was a profoundly satisfying experience, and it helped me regain the creativity that had felt elusive while I struggled to survive both cancer and the chemo and radiation treatments that poisoned me and sapped my motivation to make meaningful art. It was magical to watch the same art that had kept me inspired through the hell of chemo now pouring out of a musician. To witness another art form and to see songs coming to life in the studio felt deeply meaningful to me, not only from a creative perspective but also in the friendships that formed. Each connection helped me spark and sputter back to a more "normal" life after the endless visits to oncologists and infusion rooms.

As time passed, I had many opportunities to document the musical process, first in recording studios and then live on tour. Watching musicians perform or record, I would lock into a connection with the creators, enabling me to go back into that fly-on-the-wall observer space I felt so comfortable in as a photographer. I watched as songs took shape, the same music that moved me so much when I needed it most.

It was enlightening to witness the process of how much energy and time was necessary to complete an album. It can take years to finish an LP with all of the bad takes, redos, mistakes, and scrapped song ideas that go into creating a final body of work for a record. Being there as part of that creative process made me realize how much goes into producing a meaningful work of art, and like much of social media, most albums are carefully curated so you cannot see all the blemishes and behind-the-scenes effort. Even at the pinnacle of the game, artists can feel stuck for a long time before they return to that ineffable and affirming flow state. The creative process is challenging at all levels, no matter how established an artist. That is the beautiful struggle that is art. When you are stuck, finding the depth you seek feels impossible . . . yet when it flows, the process is almost effortless.

My time collaborating with musicians has helped me be more patient in my own creative endeavors, especially in film projects that can take many months or years to bring to fruition. There were parallels in my own healing process as well, from the trauma of a life-threatening illness and soul-wrenching heartbreak. Patience is essential during a prolonged healing journey, and it takes vulnerability and trust in others to help you see the process through to completion.

On my birthday of all days, while on a rock climbing and surf trip in Australia in 2007, I randomly met Scott Soens, a photographer I had looked up to for many years. I loved his eye for portraiture and cinematography—he had shot Jack Johnson's first couple of album covers and filmed the Malloy surf flicks *Shelter* and *180° South*, among many others. Scott was visiting our mutual friends at the surf house in Noosa where I was staying, and after introducing himself, he asked my friends, "Why is Ben Moon's hard drive here? I love that guy's work."

"That's me," I answered shyly. "I've been a huge fan of yours for years." I was beyond stoked. Scott invited me to stick around and shoot with him for another ten days in Byron Bay, where I got to learn so much from him, including advice on portraiture that I still use now. After we returned to the states, I stayed at Scott's house and slept for twenty hours straight to shake the jet lag. I groggily walked upstairs, and a guy was standing there in the kitchen wearing the exact same outfit as me, from head to toe. Same gray Patagonia jeans and brown jacket and a black "*¡Sin Represas!*" Shepard Fairey T-shirt from the *180° South* film. To top it off, we both were wearing Rainbow flip-flops.

"Uh, hey, nice outfit," I said. As he laughed and we shook hands, I realized he was Jon Swift, a brilliant yet down-to-earth astrophysicist and surfer who was featured in the *Shelter* film and who had also written "Run River," my favorite song on the soundtrack. Jon has such a relatable personality even though he is literally a genius who has worked for NASA discovering planets and stars. After our twin outfit moment, he and I ended up hanging out and becoming friends. Jon later signed a copy of the same *Shelter* film that had been donated to my benefit auction. On the cover, he scrawled *Here's to overcoming*.

This simple message of encouragement, especially from someone I had looked up to for so long, made me pause. Life had held so much struggle over the past five years, yet I was now experiencing serendipitous connections with a regularity that felt magical. I had been utterly determined to survive the divorce and cancer and setbacks, but now I felt like I was shedding all of that struggle. One step at a time, I was becoming the human I knew always existed but never believed I deserved to be. My life journey had so many mysterious twists and turns along the way, and now I was learning how to truly thrive, scars and all.

Thank you, Denali. . . . for always believing in me when no one else did, even myself.

It was two full years out from chemo when I stopped at a friend's house on a road trip. She was dating a musician named Luke Reynolds, now in the longtime rock band Guster, who was playing guitar for Brett Dennen at the time. Luke and I became fast friends, sharing common interests in music and the outdoors, and even a birthday. I had stepped away from shooting rock climbers and had started photographing Brett's shows. I had so much fun hanging with him and the crew that Brett invited me to come out on tour with them.

This was the fall of 2008, when the Canon 5D Mark II camera body was first released, the first professional DSLR camera to also shoot high-quality video, a move that revolutionized the filmmaking world almost overnight. I had shot and edited one music video about ocean plastics using a crappy camcorder I had bought from Costco. But I never dreamed of ever actually making films, as the cost of 16 mm film and professional digital video cameras was so prohibitive. Besides, I was a self-taught photographer, so how could I ever dream of working in film?

As I left to meet up with Brett Dennen and his band, I hugged Denali and told him I would only be gone for ten days. "Be good for Robert," I told Denali. Robert, my studio manager at the time, had offered to hang out with Denali while I was on tour. Brett's first show of the tour was at the Crystal Ballroom in Portland. I ran up the VIP aisle toward the stage, exhilarated to see my friends play and for the tour dates ahead.

I had heard a lot of hype about the groundbreaking video capabilities of my new camera. I switched it over to video mode. I was using a wide-angle prime lens, shooting it at the largest aperture setting because of the dim lighting, which created a depth of field that stunned me. It was like the still photographs I loved to capture were now moving, and I was able to record those moments fully, exactly how they felt to me. The unexpected entrance into the world of film and motion has opened up so many doors and led me to telling this story today. Making films has added a depth to my creative practice and taught me the value of collaboration, how the sum can be so much greater than its parts.

Although Denali was not allowed on tour, he was always on location during my photo and video shoots with bands. His presence put self-conscious musicians at ease as I snapped photos and adjusted the lighting. While I was filming with Blind Pilot at Type Foundry, a recording studio in Portland with incredible, naturally lit studios, Denali often walked through the frame as the camera rolled. True to form, he found a way to make a cameo appearance in the final videos, preparing for his final gesture of love to the world, the *Denali* film.

———

FIVE YEARS AFTER I COMPLETED MY CANCER TREATMENTS, MY DOCTORS were hopeful that my cancer would not return. More importantly, my strength had returned, and I no longer felt hampered by lingering effects of chemo or hormonal imbalances. I also was feeling much more positive emotionally, lifted up by the new friendships that had formed since my return to Portland. Those connections extended to my older friendships as well. My friend Katie was struggling through some relationship issues and life challenges. During my darkest moments in the cancer battle, Katie had been there for me, so it seemed like the perfect opportunity to repay that kindness during her own healing process. I offered to fly her out so we could sit together in an ayahuasca ceremony with my shaman Keith, who had also helped me stay alive by offering nurturing acupuncture treatments during my chemo, free of charge.

The first night, as I lay on my pile of blankets next to hers, I viscerally experienced every feeling she was going through as she fought letting go. Fear, anxiety, apprehension, self-loathing. It was painful for me, but I cannot imagine what she was enduring. I offered up as much love and energy as I could to support her.

An hour passed and Katie still was not feeling any effects from the medicine. She whispered over to me, "Screw this, I'm out of here," and fled the room. After a few moments, Keith and I went outside to check on her and found her lying in my car, curled up next to Denali. Keith tried to convince her to come back in and join the circle, but Katie firmly said, "*No.* Go away, this won't work, nothing works for me."

I lay there contemplating her struggles as I gradually felt the medicine come on. An hour later while Keith closed the ceremony, I felt myself dropping in, but I was unable to speak or ask for help. What followed was the most intense psychedelic experience of my life. For the next six hours I lay on my side, having intense visuals that faced all of my childhood fears of war, death, and loneliness. I saw mothers in bombed-out towns, cradling their babies to protect them. It was horrifying, but I was well aware that it was a visual representation of the fear and anxiety I had felt about war while growing up. It was profoundly healing to begin to understand those fears.

The next night, Katie drank the ayahuasca willingly, ready to come to terms with her own fears. An hour after each of the ten ceremony participants had consumed a small glass of the medicine, Keith summoned each person to come and sit facing him while he worked with them one-on-one. When Katie's turn came, as soon as she sat down I sensed she was letting go. I heard her crying softly and then breaking down completely, sobbing uncontrollably for nearly an hour.

Oh no, I thought, *she's going to hate me for this, she's having a miserable experience, and especially after her not wanting to participate last night.*

I sat there, in my little nest of blankets and pillows, and tried to send her as much support as I could. She began to calm, and after Keith wrapped up his work with her, Katie came back and lay down on her blanket beside me. She reached over, and grabbed my hand, holding it for a long while as if to say *thank you*. On the ride home the next morning, she confided that the night had brought her so much clarity about her patterns surrounding men and relationships.

"So, you're glad you went?" I asked. "You don't hate me for dragging you in there? I was trying to help, but you seemed miserable!"

"Yes. Thank you so much for this opportunity and for putting up with me! And for wanting to help. It was such a profound night," she said.

"What did Keith say to you up there?" I asked.

"He said, 'The more you fight it, the more of a purgative it is.' So I fought it and puked, then fought it and puked even more."

"Oh wow, I'm so glad you had a profound experience! I know this type of healing and therapy is so hard to describe, it means a lot that you trusted me enough to come out for this."

As we drove, I reflected on my own healing journey, from cancer, heartbreak, and mental illness. This path had been forged by a series of small gestures from friends, Denali, and others who lifted me up. I never could have made it this far without the support and encouragement of loved ones, especially when I was at my lowest. Watching Katie take this small step forward in her own process showed me the value of helping others. A timely and kind nudge can motivate someone toward a different future.

———

AT THE PORTLAND PREMIERE OF *180° SOUTH*, I MET UP WITH JEFF JOHNSON and Chris Malloy backstage, when Isaac Brock, lead singer of Modest Mouse, rolled up with Lisa, his new girlfriend, whom I had dated for a brief time earlier. I had heard rumors of Isaac's temper, so I cringed as he extended his hand and introduced himself. Instead of being angry, he was courteous and kind. After the film screened, Emmett and Chris Malloy—two film directors I respected immensely—invited me to come to the after-party at Isaac's home.

I was on a bike, so I arrived ahead of everyone else, and as I walked up the steps to the front door, I saw Lisa disappear upstairs with an armload of freshly laundered bedding. Hesitantly, I knocked and came inside. I had just removed my boots and messenger bag when Isaac emerged from the other room.

"What the hell do you think you're doing?" he said.

"Uh, so sorry, man. Chris told me there was a party here."

"No, dude, they bailed. We're going to bed. You should leave and go home."

Deflated, I couldn't get my boots on quickly enough. My heart raced as I headed for the door. I felt a slap on my back, and I turned to see his eyes dancing with amusement.

"Consider yourself fucked with!" He laughed.

I allowed myself to breathe for the first time and exhaled with relief that he was messing with me, a cruel joke, considering the circumstances. He invited me to stay, offering me a drink and a tour of his eclectic home that could have doubled as a museum.

Hours passed and many drinks were consumed with the cast

and crew of *180° South*. I was admiring the odd curios along the walls and saw a pair of boxing gloves. Picking one up, Isaac looked at me and said, "You wanna go?"

Lisa shook her head with concern, but Isaac was undeterred and led me to his kitchen, where he pulled on the gloves in front of his mom, stepdad, Lisa, Jeff, Chris, and Emmett. It was a surreal moment, to be in a circle of my film, photography, and music heroes, standing toe-to-toe with a rock star whose songs were the soundtrack through my years at Metolius.

Isaac stood in front of a row of cabinets with glass doors. To my right, his mom and stepfather were standing next to a pot of soup heating on the cookstove. He danced side to side and took a few mock swings before rushing at me with a flurry of punches. I warded off as many as I could, trying to rationalize and make sense of this truly bizarre scenario. *Could I actually punch him right here in front of his mom and girlfriend? And my personal heroes, the Malloys? What if I break a cabinet or hurt him?*

Isaac swung and connected on a few rapid blows, and I started to see stars. *What if Isaac knocks me out?* I thought. Lisa lifted Isaac's right arm, declaring him the victor of round one. "Let's go again," I said, adrenaline rushing and my ego feeling worse for wear. We tapped gloves and began circling each other. I was more aggressive this time, and landed a punch squarely to his jaw, knocking his hat off and sending him stumbling backward. He was several inches shorter than me and had a foot less reach, but I felt I had to return the favor and save a bit of my pride. It felt like an initiation ritual of sorts, trading blows with a rock star in front of those who had inspired my filmmaking and who had also created film and music that had helped me through my darkest days.

Later, Isaac and I ran into each other in the produce aisle at the local grocer. Isaac grabbed my arm and clenched my biceps. "Dude, you're jacked! You could've hit me way harder. You were holding back, weren't you?"

A few years later, he would call and offer support during the most painful day of my life, the day Denali took his last breath.

FIVE YEARS AFTER MY LAST CHEMO TREATMENT, I RECEIVED A CALL FROM *Outside* magazine to shoot with the not-yet-famous rock climber but still-legendary free soloist Alex Honnold. I had been published in the magazine several times over the years and was ecstatic to finally land a feature story. I had known Alex through the climbing world, but we had not yet worked together, so I was excited for the prospect, especially on a story for a more mainstream magazine about the outdoor world.

Alex had climbed Moonlight Buttress in Zion National Park and Half Dome's Regular Northwest Face route, both without ropes, and was becoming notorious for his calculated yet bold ropeless climbs. This was prior to the *60 Minutes* interview that launched Alex into the limelight, nearly a decade before his recent audacious and awe-inspiring free solo of El Capitan's Freerider route. This utterly astonishing athletic feat was documented in the Oscar-winning documentary *Free Solo*, a film that screened for months in theaters and brought both rock climbing and Alex to the public eye.

After years of traveling as a rock climber, Alex decided in 2012 to start a nonprofit whose mission was to bring solar power to communities without access to electricity to improve quality of life. For the first few years, he shifted a staggering 30 percent of his income to the nonprofit. I remember Alex telling me, while at the Mountainfilm festival, about the foundation, shrugging before stating matter-of-factly, "I make more money than I need. I mean, I live in my van." I was struck by his perspective. Years later, we would both become ambassadors for a new electric adventure vehicle manufacturer called Rivian, eventually partnering up to make a film about using repurposed electric vehicle batteries to create microgrids in Adjuntas, a mountain community in Puerto Rico that was without power for nearly a year after Hurricane Maria.

For the *Outside* magazine article, Alex and I shot for a week together at Smith Rock. It was a joy to revisit those canyons that I had spent eleven years exploring, and I photographed Alex on several of my favorite aesthetic lines. One afternoon we were rained out from climbing, so we shot portraits at a friend's house. I was running out of ideas, so I asked that he go shirtless and suspend himself from the ceiling by pinching the exposed beams with his bare hands. Alex still jokes that I was the first photographer that ever got him to go shirtless.

For the final location I photographed him soloing routes at Trout Creek, a columnar basalt buttress high up on a central Oregon plateau revered for its spectacular traditional climbing. The cracks we ascended were often formed where huge basalt pillars, six feet wide and fifty feet long, had fallen from the wall before resting neatly on the hillside, forming perfect platforms to belay from or hang out on. The surrounding area is well known by fly fishermen who wade into the flowing waters of the Deschutes River, which splits the landscape all the way to the horizon, where Mount Jefferson allows your gaze to rest while admiring the spectacular sunsets from the prime viewing location on the fallen flat basalt columns.

On a hot high-desert afternoon, my photography assistant and I were walking with Denali along the flat two-track back to the camp-ground when the distinctive warning rattle of a rattlesnake shattered the peaceful sound of rushing waters from the river below. The rattle startled me, and I leaped away from the angry fanged coil with an al-most superhuman reflex, traveling nine feet to my right in a split second, all while shouldering a sixty-pound backpack stuffed with rock climb-ing hardware, ropes, camera bodies, and heavy lenses. While midair, I tapped a foot to the ground to alter my course while in flight, tackling Denali as he lunged toward the threat. Tangled up with me on the ground, he gave me a look that conveyed both surprise and disgust.

> Why in the world did you stop me? I was only protecting you.

A bite to Denali's face or neck likely would have been fatal to him in his headlong rush to disarm the attacker. "Thanks, D," I said grate-fully, hugging him tightly as the snake slithered away. "I realize you were protecting me, but if that meant losing you . . . I'm not sure I could've lived with the pain of you being gone."

> I would do it for you again, any day! I've got your back, my friend.

10

Another Wave

Despite the shift in focus in my photography toward human emotion, I continued to embrace opportunities to document athletes interacting with nature in its more extreme forms. I refused to let the physical challenge of living with a colostomy hold me back and welcomed any opportunity to push the limitations of my condition.

In October 2010, a massive groundswell from the west put me, myself, and Earl through the ultimate test. I had been invited to shoot a big wave contest at Nelscott Reef, a rocky shelf a half mile offshore from Lincoln City, Oregon. Thoughts of the contest woke me at two o'clock in the morning, and I checked the buoys online to see how big the swell had become.

The buoy read:

25 FEET AT 19 SECONDS

I was stunned. This meant potential for waves breaking well over fifty feet out on the reef, something that had never been seen before at an Oregon surfing contest.

Later that morning, the waves were breaking over the reef with forty-five- to sixty-five-foot faces. Several of the Jet Skis were wrecked, surfboards were lost and broken, and a few big-wave-veteran surfers chose to sit out the contest later in the day. In the afternoon hours, I caught a ride out to the reef on a Jet Ski to shoot the event. I was in awe of this rare display of nature's raw power, as massive avalanches of storm-swell energy rumbled around me.

I had been shooting photographs from one of the remaining Jet Skis, and after another broke down, I swapped drivers and was left sitting on the malfunctioning watercraft behind Tao Berman, a world-class kayaker famous for his ninety-eight-foot kayak drops, more familiar with rivers and waterfalls than the waves and currents of the ocean. I realized that our watercraft was having serious issues and was operating at far less than its normal power, and my heart sank.

A series of unfortunate events left me at the mercy of the largest swell ever surfed in Oregon history. As the contestants and their support crews and photographers sat in the relative safety of a channel between two rocky reef shelves, a massive set of waves closed out the entire channel and took everyone off guard as skis sped north toward the shoulder of the wave, scrambling for safety.

As Tao guided our Jet Ski straight up the face of the first wave in what would turn out to be a monstrous set, the ski began to falter and stalled out. Instead of pointing toward the wave's shoulder where the wave was not yet breaking, as the more experienced watermen from

Hawaii, Brazil, and Australia had just done, he made an ill-informed decision to turn and try to outrun the wave.

We were swiftly overtaken, and as we approached the trough in front of the wave, I felt the engine falter again just as the massive leading edge of the wave broke right behind us, emitting a concussive roar and giving my heart a fear I had never felt before or in the years since. I knew that simply to survive this encounter would require divine intervention. Yet, in spite of the sheer terror of it all, I was oddly at peace. There was simply no margin for error—to panic meant death.

As the mountainous wave exploded behind us, a ninety-foot-high wall of white water engulfed us both like the blade of a snowplow. Tao yelled, "Hold on!" as the backwash lifted us, and we were thrown into the air. I watched as the Jet Ski was tossed over my head, and I could see Tao ten feet below me. I was slammed into him in a pile-driving action that would have been comically like pro wrestling if we were not facing this raw power of the sea. A split second after I landed on Tao, the Jet Ski crashed down, driving into my shoulder and slamming me underwater. Had that machine landed on my head instead, there is no question that I would have been knocked unconscious and drowned.

I was swallowed by the breaking wave and experienced indescribable hydraulic forces underwater. I was folded and tossed and torn with such force that three days later I would still feel as if all my internal organs had been individually smashed with a sledgehammer. I was taking the beating of my life.

Three more enormous waves followed in almost uniform precision at nineteen-second intervals, and as I gasped for air after surfacing from the fourth hold-down, I was keenly aware that if there was a fifth wave in the set, this breath would be my last. The air seemed to go calm, my senses trancelike as time slowed and the sky deepened its shade of blue.

Another wave did not materialize, and there was a merciful lull. I struggled desperately to clear the foam that lay on the surface of the aerated water, making it hard to see or take in a full breath without choking. Tao yelled out, "Are you okay?" and calmly admitted the gravity of our situation. "No one's coming for us with another ski, they think we went all the way to shore. We have to swim in ourselves."

I stared at the sky and saw a single-engine Cessna circling high above. Earlier I had turned down a seat in that plane because I wanted to be in the water with the surfers, to feel and capture the intensity and camaraderie of the contest from sea level. *That looks so warm and comfortable*, I thought. *Why didn't I take the seat?* I thought of Denali, curled up in the bed in the back of my Element, and wished desperately that I could just take one more nap with him nuzzled on my chest.

Photographing this contest came with risk, but I had not considered the possibility that things could go so awry. There was only one safety ski still running during the contest, which was inadequate under the best of circumstances. No one even knew we were in trouble. The safety team and the other surfers just assumed we went back to shore. *I survived cancer! Will it really end like this?* I screamed silently.

As we began the long swim to safety, the strong currents of the heaving, twenty-five-foot beach break nearer to shore began to pull at us with a strength that surprised us both. Tao screamed, "Swim!" and rapidly stroked, angling away from the latest danger. Somehow, I was still holding my camera in its big waterproof housing, perhaps because it gave this insane situation a bit of normalcy, a reason to be out there. I considered ditching it but had no time and instead swam with every shred of strength I had left with my legs and one free arm. Without the swim fins I had decided not to wear, my efforts were meager. As I dove through the lip of the largest wave of the set, my PFD kept me too close to the surface, and I felt a sickening sensation as the bottom dropped out and I free-fell twenty feet toward the rocks. I closed my eyes and waited for my now-certain end, slamming into the water mere feet from a motor home–sized rock that I would later learn had totaled our Jet Ski. The inside of my left foot struck the water first, wrenching my knee and tearing the medial collateral ligament.

As I bodysurfed toward the seemingly still-distant shore, I shielded my face and head with my arms to avoid smashing into rocks obscured by the heaps of foam swirling around in the chaotic currents. Ten minutes later my feet made contact with the sandy bottom, and the realization that I would live began to sink in. Tao was nowhere in sight, and as I began, oddly enough, to calmly accept that he might not have made it, he popped up down the beach, almost screaming with elation, "Now I know I can swim through fifty-foot surf, isn't that amazing?!" In shock, I stared at him blankly as he continued, "Did you ever think you were going to really die?" I held up two fingers and meekly admitted, "Yeah, twice." "Twice?" he howled with glee. "Wasn't that amazing?!" It seemed as if he wanted to swim back out and relive the experience.

Later, I learned that throughout Tao's career, his utter confidence in himself has given him an uncanny ability to suppress his fear. For him, our near-death experience was nothing short of a thrill ride. But the surfers who have experienced Nelscott's massive swells always reacted far differently. After I retold the story to Gerry Lopez, he calmly explained how the slabby nature of a wave like Nelscott will hold you in the dangerous impact zone for far longer than a wave like Pe'ahi (also known as Jaws) on the north shore of Maui, which circulated you quickly out the back. Then his eyes narrowed with anger and he said, "They could've killed you. That should never have happened. Next time you call me, bro, I'll drive your Jet Ski."

When Tao and I first exited the water, we had no clue where we were and walked a set of stairs that led up the cliff face to a cluster of houses at the top. A crowd had gathered, and the first person I saw was Sam Beebe, a friend who had been shooting photographs from the cliff of the two swimmers struggling for shore. He had no way of knowing it was me.

Surprised to see him, I hoarsely whispered, "Sam?!" and broke down into tears as the gravity of the experience began to set in. It is difficult to describe the forces of a swell that powerful, but it must be similar to being tossed haplessly about by a tornado, only underwater. It was the most intense forty-five minutes of my life, yet facing mortality so acutely instilled an involuntary calm, a deep acceptance that I was in no way in control of my fate. With cancer there was time to panic, long hours for the dark tensions of anxiety to fully set in, but in those waves, it was so Zen-like. To panic there was to lose valuable oxygen and drown, or to inhale aerated water and choke and drown. Panicking simply was not an option.

I attempted to shrug off the experience while chatting with the surfers who had competed in the event, but as exhaustion set in, I realized that I needed time alone. After stumbling back to my car, I found Denali waiting patiently. Raising an eyebrow as he looked on with concern, he let out a deep sigh. My guard crumbled and the tears started to flow as I hugged him tightly and took in my first true full breath since being consumed by the waves.

Days later I still felt as if I had been run over by a bulldozer, and only then did I realize how deeply I'd been in shock. Denali observed me with a keen eye in the days following the accident, sensing the deep trauma I had not yet acknowledged. He always knew things, often well before I ever had a clue.

> You're in pain, but something else is wrong . . . You're so jumpy at every little sound, and you seem on edge and just not yourself. Please don't leave me behind, I need to be with you to make sure you're okay.

This near drowning was a more focused, intense brush with mortality, whereas cancer is an extended version of that. Within the massive forces of the sea, I lived second to second, and in facing cancer I battled the disease minute to minute, hour to hour, day to day, month to month. Rarely could I see beyond a span of a day as the burden of the upcoming toxic treatments would be too much to bear.

The post-traumatic stress from both experiences lasted for years, every hint of illness or headache becoming a potential new tumor growth, every wave tumbling in front of me in the surf causing a similar wide-eyed panic.

During a heavy swell in the Lofoten Islands in Norway five years later, I was hyperventilating intensely, paddling hard for the horizon far beyond where surfers lined up at the break, before my friend yelled, "Ben! Where are you going?" and snapped me out of my confused trance.

Healing from any major trauma can take many years, or a lifetime if left unresolved. Each wave I have paddled into since has brought me closer to making peace with the big-wave experience, and every cancer-free breath I draw assures me that my tumor no longer is a threat.

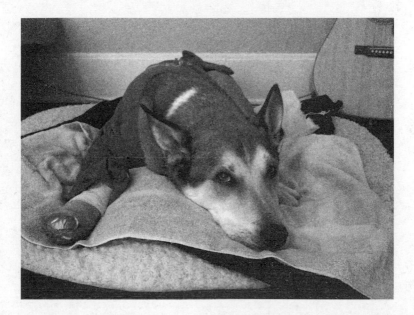

11

Denali's Battle

On an overcast Portland morning in May 2009, I was sitting on the back porch drinking yerba maté, procrastinating on the huge photo edit that was due for a client. I stroked Denali's back, relishing a moment of quiet connection with my best friend before I sat in front of a screen for the next six hours. Denali was nine and a half years old, yet still an agile and capable athlete. He and I would often run long sections of the forested trails nearby, doing ten-mile loops with ease within the eighty-mile trail system of Portland's 5,200-acre Forest Park.

As I tousled his fur, I felt a lump on Denali's side, just a few inches to the right of his spine. I suddenly felt cold, fully aware that the lump had not been there before. I called his veterinary office immediately, and they said they could see us right away.

As Denali and I walked those two short blocks to the clinic just around the corner from our apartment, my heart became heavy with dread. Denali was unfazed, tugging on his leash in anticipation of the treats that awaited him. He was a favorite patient of the veterinary assistants, and he turned on the charm for some tasty snacks. Denali was continually motivated by his northern-dog appetite, even though I had never trained him with food or treats. If I had, he would have had a repertoire of a thousand tricks.

During the exam, the vet took a biopsy of the lump, then found three other smaller tumors, one of them on his right front paw. The biopsy confirmed my worst fears; all four were mast cell tumors.

Denali had cancer.

My face felt numb as the room blurred. Was this my fault? How did this happen? In the confusion, I heard the vet speaking through the high-pitched whine of blood rushing to my ears.

"The tumor on Denali's front right paw is a concern. I am not sure we will be able to get a safe margin without amputating his leg. Three-legged dogs can get around just fine." *Denali, an amputee? He's an athlete! No way.* I was stunned, feeling the guilt pour in.

That afternoon, Denali and I ran his favorite trails, and I gave him all the love and treats I could muster. He slept curled up close to me, under my arm all night. I doubt I gave him a choice, but he was happy to oblige.

The next morning, as the vet techs prepped Denali for his proce-dure, I pleaded with the veterinarian to do everything he could to save Denali's life. "If you can keep him on all four legs, he and I will both be forever grateful!" Denali was my rock, my pillar, the one I leaned on heavily for my identity and well-being. How could he support me if he had only three legs?

What if the cancer had already entered his lymph nodes . . . or worse yet, his organs? How could I survive if he passed on before his time? He seemed so strong just weeks ago!

How would I ever forgive myself for not catching the symptoms sooner? I had been in denial about my own cancer and it very nearly cost me my life, but to let Denali suffer a similar fate felt unforgivable.

When I brought him home after the procedure, I was shocked by all the bandages. A huge swath of skin, eleven inches in diameter, had been removed from one side, and another four inches had been removed from the other. "I love you, D. . . . I am here for you, no matter what it takes. And I am so grateful you still have all four legs," I murmured. I carried him to my Honda Element and laid him gently into the camping bed I had built in the cargo area. Groggily, he looked up. His eyes tried to focus on mine as he licked my hand.

> Thank you, my friend. I feel so woozy. And I hurt
> everywhere. But you're with me, so everything will be okay.

After the anesthesia began to wear off, Denali tried to stand up and cried loudly, whimpering in pain. His eyes were wide as he looked around, and he seemed confused by the intensity of the unfamiliar sensation. The incisions and shaved square patches checkered his coat, looking not unlike the aerial views of many Oregon forests, with clearcuts marring the landscape. In one area on his back, the sutures and staples strained against the tension of the skin that remained along his spine.

As Denali hobbled forward, the cone he wore to prevent licking caught on the door frame, and he was knocked backward onto his haunches. His pitiful expression showed only hopelessness and despair, and I ran to hold him as I sobbed into his fur. "You're going to be okay, my friend, I'll never leave your side, I swear it."

———

THAT NIGHT I SLEPT ON THE FUTON IN OUR LIVING ROOM, MY HEAD RESTING against his. Despite the prescription painkillers, he would cry out in pain every few minutes, each whimper tearing at my heart as I struggled to make him comfortable. In those long, dark hours of the early morning, I promised him that I would never, ever let him suffer. "When it's your time to go, just tell me, all right? Please just let me know."

Denali always had my back during my lowest points during chemo and was unwavering when I could barely get out of bed. How could I repay that sort of loyalty? I lay awake recalling all our good times and laughed at the situations Denali and I had found ourselves in. "You're gonna bounce back from this, D, I know you will."

Denali was resilient and a fighter who was not ready to leave my side. The removal of the four tumors took a few months to fully heal, especially the largest of the incisions on his back. Our ten-mile runs became slow walks around the block, with Denali wearing one of my old T-shirts to protect the sutures, and a Ruffwear dog boot on the foot that he thankfully still had full use of. Ruffwear later sent Denali a soft-shell jacket, a major style upgrade from the T-shirt, which kept him from licking his staples. Gradually he regained strength and mobility and proved his resilience by bouncing back remarkably well. Denali never quite returned to his previous physical form after that ordeal, yet his enthusiasm for being outside for an adventure never waned.

12

Slowing Down

To be an adventure photographer, or any professional photographer for that matter, means being continually on the move. Over Denali's rich life span, I always tried to limit my trips to lengths of two or three weeks at most, unless he could join me. While many of my peers took pride in being home for only three months a year, spending months in the Himalayas or jet-setting from one assignment or commercial gig to the next, I was more selective with which jobs I accepted in order for Denali and me to spend more time together. Only twice during his life did I make exceptions, on prolonged trips to Kauai and Australia. Both were opportunities that were crucial in my career and personal growth and seemed worth the temporary separation. This decision would not have been possible without the trusted friends who loved Denali enough to care for him while I was gone.

After the surgery to remove Denali's cancerous tumors, signs of his age and the wear and tear from the procedures started to become evident. Prior to his cancer surgery, he could run ten miles with me and rarely lag. Denali was slowing down considerably, so I adjusted our adventures together to make sure he was comfortable. An uncomfortable wakeup call about his limitations came when he was eleven, while we were hiking up the back side of the Stawamus Chief in Squamish, British Columbia. Halfway to the summit, Denali's breathing became noisy, his eyes were wide, and he visibly gasped for air. Tourists stared while he rasped loudly with each breath as he labored to get enough oxygen. At first, I did not recognize the severity of the situation, and I encouraged Denali to continue, letting him rest every few minutes. I thought he was just fatigued, and could not imagine Denali not wanting to make it to the summit with me.

As we continued upward, the seriousness of the situation became more obvious. Denali would not make it to the top, and if we carried on, he might collapse from the exertion. This realization was shocking to me. It was a stark illustration of his aging, a signal that my willing sidekick who had followed me everywhere for the past decade with such energy and grace was now going to have to stay behind on many adventures.

Denali and I sat down to rest at a viewpoint overlooking the turquoise waters of the Howe Sound. He was still breathing heavily, wheezing against some unseen obstacle in his throat. Denali leaned into me, and as I stroked his coat, my mind reeled with the fresh reality that "our" adventures would become "my" adventures. This was nearly too difficult a concept for me to grasp. I had depended on Denali through every challenging experience for over a decade. Where would I find the strength without him at my side?

We stayed in Squamish for another week, and Denali stayed behind at the house while Sonnie and I finished putting up a new route on the Squamish Buttress. For five long days, he and I worked feverishly to clean a three-pitch variation to the standard route up the

Chief, creating an option up an awkward section of the wall that stymied most beginners. It was intense manual labor but rewarding work high up above the valley floor.

To celebrate the completion of our efforts, a route called North Face of Squamish Buttress (also known as Butt Light or the Butt Face by locals), Sonnie invited six other elite climbers to join us on a free solo of the entire 1,800-foot-tall formation from the ground up. The hardest move on the entire climb is rated only 5.9, well below everyone's ability, so we moved quickly as a group up the slabby Apron formation, with only our chalk bags and the beers we stashed in them to weigh us down. We climbed casually, laughing and goofing around as we ascended. I often had to remind myself to stay focused as none of us were roped up, and one slip could send a few of us hurtling to the ground a thousand feet below. As we started up the section that Sonnie and I had just opened up, Alex Honnold went first and shouted down, "Wow, this is really good climbing!" Alex has no filter and tells it exactly like it is, so we took this as the ultimate compliment for the energy we exerted over the past week.

All eight of us stood on the summit only forty-five minutes after leaving the parking lot. As we took in the view, Tim Emmett, a British-born climber and BASE jumper, joked, "All we need now is eight parachutes!" It took us longer to descend the trail back to the cars than it had to climb from the base to the summit of the wall.

After Denali and I returned home from Canada, I called Denali's vet to discuss his breathing condition. Denali was diagnosed with laryngeal paralysis, which basically meant that his vocal cords were not getting out of the way during his breathing as they normally would. This paralysis was literally suffocating him.

I thought back to my promise to never let him suffer and wondered aloud if the condition was causing him pain. "Is surgery a viable option for a dog of Denali's age?" I asked.

"The procedure is expensive, but many dogs can have a full recovery. There is a danger of inhaling water while drinking and swimming because their built-in defense mechanism has been altered. Pneumonia will always be a concern." I was torn over whether it would be wise to put Denali through another surgery, as he had been in so much pain following the removal of his four mast cell tumors.

I debated this for a couple of months and could not take his asthma-like symptoms any longer. I felt the benefits of the surgery outweighed the risks if it meant Denali could regain some of his old vigor and strength. I was tight on funds, and just as I wondered aloud how to pay for the procedure, I got a call from Patagonia asking me to film trail running for a half day over in Bend. I have learned over and over that if I focus on a positive outcome of a seemingly impossible scenario, the details will take care of themselves. During the three-hour drive to the location for the shoot, I repeated the mantra "This one's for you, D! Love you, bro."

It was heartrending to watch the vet techs once again prep Denali for surgery. Nearly every time I had been under general anesthesia for my cancer surgeries, the drugs had made me sick, and I worried it would be too much for his weakened twelve-year-old immune system to handle. As the IVs were inserted, I stroked his head and reassured him that this would help him breathe and we would be able to take to the trails together again.

Miraculously, and despite his age, the surgery was much less stressful for Denali than the previous one to remove his cancerous tumors had been. The week following surgery, he rapidly improved. As his body was no longer oxygen starved, his face seemed to lose years of strain and his breathing was steady and relaxed. It reminded me of the transformation I had seen in my own face after letting go of toxic relationships that had visibly aged me.

Denali and I continued to explore together, but our exploits became more limited and the pace slower. In spite of Denali's physical limitations, I still made daily efforts to get him out to his favorite places. Before I would bring him, I would make sure the weather was comfortable, not too hot or cold to stress his system.

After Denali's fourteenth birthday, I brought him to Smith Rock to hang as my friend, Shanjean, and I climbed Tsunami, a steep route rated 5.12c that I had bolted during the van days. I knew full well that this might be the last time Denali would join me.

Hiking the steep trail out of Smith Rock to the parking lot normally took about twenty minutes, but by that point in the day the slog was a challenge for Denali's veteran hips. At his unhurried, meandering pace I recognized that it could take more than an hour. I decided to pick him up and gently carry him, draping his body over my shoulders so his once-muscular frame could rest evenly over my back and on my climbing pack. His sixty pounds added to my already thirty-pound climbing pack, but it was a minimal burden to shoulder so that I could still climb with my old friend and favorite crag companion.

———

OUR ADVENTURES OUTSIDE BECAME LESS FREQUENT, ESPECIALLY IN THE heat of summer. I took photography jobs closer and closer to home, and life's pace became slower, the sniffing walks around our Portland neighborhood going from ten blocks, to five, to three. Denali's gait grew increasingly unsteady, but our bond remained steadfast.

Denali always loved to pick raspberries, and my Portland backyard was a veritable smorgasbord for his appetite . . . plums, figs, apricots, strawberries, thornless blackberries, three varieties of cherries, peaches, Asian pears, and nectarines. During his final summer, he ate every single strawberry before they began to ripen. He cleaned out all the low-hanging cherries and devoured plum and fig drops. I laughed out loud during Denali's prolonged tug-of-war with the Asian pear tree branch, his shaky haunches straining when the tree refused to release its unripe fruits for him. He did not give up, tugging until the branch's grip failed and he was able to eat the fruit.

The only human food I ever gave him was the juice from tuna and sardine cans, and the occasional apple core, yet his northern-dog genes never allowed him a reprieve from his obsession with filling his stomach. While hiking the trail that skirted the base of the climbs at Smith Rock, Denali would find apple cores that climbers had discarded wedged and hidden in between chunks of basalt in the retaining walls.

Years later, when his hearing began to fail, he was nearly deaf yet always aware if I was anywhere near the kitchen. Utterly unresponsive to my verbal cues, he would still appear every time a can opener popped the seal on a can of tuna, or the lid on a tin of sardines was peeled back.

My grandfather Art, on my mom's side, had that same selective hearing later in life. "*Art!* Did you *hear*?" my grandmother would yell across the room. After the third time, he would respond, "Oh, *Helen*. I *heard* you."

I came to realize that as his pace slowed, Denali was teaching me patience, to relax and savor each moment. Instead of questioning why aging had to be so hard, I began to relish the simplicity of our routine and the humor in his old man quirks. Our ten-mile runs diminished to ten steps down the block, yet Denali's enthusiasm for those ten steps and the odors he could drink in from of every blade of grass and branch remained the same.

"How will I know when it's time?" became a constant thought. I prayed he would go out with grace and style. When I traveled, I worried that he would pass while I was out of town, but deep down, I knew he would not let go without me by his side.

13

Going Alone

During the summer of 2013, which was to be Denali's last, he was still getting around, albeit more slowly. His hearing had finally begun to fail, although at times it still seemed like he might just be stubbornly *pretending* not to hear. On the Fourth of July, I was packing up the car to camp out on the coast and left the screen door propped open. Denali never wore his collar at night, so as he roamed the house collarless, in a moment true to his personality, he slipped outside to the street while my back was turned.

As I glanced around the house, I felt a panic well up in my chest. Denali was gone. No collar, nearly deaf, on the most reviled day of the year for dogs. *The fireworks!* I thought. *I have to find him now or I will never see him again.*

More dogs go stray and run away on the Fourth of July than on any other day. A wave of guilt, then nausea washed over me. *I've lost Denali and this time it's all on me.* I sprinted around the block, hollering his name. I knew that, even if he heard me, he would be determined to follow through on his mission: to make friends and find tasty snacks using whatever means necessary. I grabbed my bike and did a few frantic laps around the neighborhood.

I choked back tears as I realized I may never find him, especially if someone set off a massive illegal firework, a commonplace occurrence in Oregon that time of year, even in Portland neighborhoods. Taking a deep breath, I walked around the block one more time and caught a whiff of steaks on a grill. I followed the scent to a backyard barbecue, and sure enough, there was Denali sitting in the midst of a group of people, getting petted and loved on. He did not see me approach as he was fixated on the grill, dreaming of bratwurst and T-bone steaks.

Soon after that incident, he suffered from a terrifying bout of idiopathic peripheral vestibular disease, also called old dog vestibular disease. In dogs and most mammals, the vestibular system is responsible for balance and spatial awareness. A malfunction of this system will induce vertigo, that disorienting feeling where things look like they are moving when they are not.

Dogs affected by this disease can have an episode that comes on without warning, causing a loss of balance, often accompanied by a head tilt and walking in circles. Many dogs are put down by their owners during attacks of this mysterious illness, as it seems that it is the sign that it is the end.

Denali and I had been playing "old man fetch" in the backyard, a slower version of the game than during days of his prime, and he approached it with the same endearing enthusiasm of a puppy. After a few tosses, Denali chased the ball, and everything went wrong. Without any premonition, his head suddenly cocked to one side, and he fell hard to the ground. I ran to his side and looked into his eyes, and they spun with confusion as he strained to focus on my face. I was terrified that he was dying right there. For the next ten days he could not stand without stumbling. It was heartbreaking to watch him vomit from the vertigo and pee the bed for the first time in his life.

Each time Denali needed to go outside to relieve himself, I had to carry him into the yard and hold him steady as I supported his weight, or he would pee all over himself. He would lie in his cot trying to rest, looking at me with a confused expression. I sobbed into his fur and prayed that he would not go in such an undignified fashion. He had been the noble banner of strength I had followed for so long, and I hoped desperately for any recovery so that he could finish his days with honor and dignity.

Frantic, I searched online for any sign of hope and found a doctor named Becky Jester, a holistic veterinarian who treated dogs with acupuncture. Dr. Jester sat with Denali in our yard, working with her needles and administering small doses of electrical stimulation to the acupressure points along Denali's spine and neck.

After an hour, Becky finished her treatment, and Denali, like Lazarus, stood up slowly, trotted over to his tennis ball, and looked at me, wagging his tail. I sobbed shameless tears of joy to see my best friend come back to life so suddenly. I could not help but wonder what was driving him to hang on.

Denali's miraculous recovery from that challenge happened a little over a year into my new relationship with a naturopathic physician and yoga instructor named Hannah. She was one of my favorite yoga teachers long before she and I began dating. I had been enamored with the graceful way she moved and the elegant poise she brought to her classes. I finally mustered the courage to ask her out. I was hopeful about this new romance, but after a few months of dating the reality of our incompatibility became apparent.

Things became even more rocky once Hannah moved in with me during Denali's final summer. One morning, I caught my reflection in the mirror. I was shocked to see how much older and how exhausted I looked. New gray hairs were a signal of the awareness that I had to leave this relationship before we crossed the threshold of no return. At first, I had found her energy and confidence irresistible. To others, we had seemed like a perfect match, a yogi naturopath and an adventure photographer. In reality, the stress and negativity that I felt while living with her was taking an immense toll on my psyche and health. I simply could not repeat the stress and negativity that manifested in my health after the dissolution of my marriage to Mel.

At night, instead of holding Hannah close to me, I slept as far away as my queen-sized mattress would allow. An extended marathon of attempting to make the relationship work became an exhausting and prolonged breakup. Characteristically, I have had an issue letting go of relationships before I have seen them through to the bitter end, so I realized breaking free of this relationship would not prove easy. We had bantered about the idea of moving to Santa Barbara to escape the Pacific Northwest's dreary winters, but I could not see myself making that sort of commitment with her.

Denali was in his final months, and a friend and midtempo trip-hop artist known as Emancipator had reached out to let me know he was opening for the electronic dance act Pretty Lights. I decided to go to the show, thinking that a night of music could offer an escape from the anxiety I felt about ending my relationship. I ate a psilocybin chocolate to offer introspection and help me lose myself in the music and light show for a few hours. I hoped that eating the mushrooms would provide some clarity on my feelings about the relationship, and that they did, with a metaphorical punch to my face. About three songs into the Pretty Lights act, I began to feel nauseated and tapped on Hannah's shoulder to tell her I needed to go find a restroom. When she turned to me to ask why I had to pee already, she was literally unrecognizable. Her visage had morphed into a face of a terrifying demon, and the sight of it nearly caused me to vomit right there. "We have to go!" I yelled over the music. "Right *now*."

The remainder of the evening I spent staring into a fire in the woodstove with Denali lying in my lap, mulling over all that had transpired and where I saw my life going. I felt immense clarity, even a lightness. A desire overcame me to purge all the clutter and unnecessary possessions that now clogged my basement. I also recognized clearly that I could not tolerate the heaviness of this relationship in my home any longer.

Earlier that same summer, Hannah suggested that I work with Tatyana, a wise counselor and mentor in her sixties in hopes that the counseling sessions would salvage our relationship. After my first phone consult with Tatyana, I realized she would transform my life for the better. She understood me immediately in a depth I had never attained with another counselor. Each ninety-minute session that followed would result in ten to twenty pages of notes in an effort to capture Tatyana's insights and wisdom.

At age thirty-nine I heard the term *empath* used for the first time, in a session with Tatyana.

She described it as such:

When someone walks into a room, most people can observe how that person is feeling by the look on their face, whether they are happy or upset or stressed. You, you're what I call an off-the-charts empath. You not only observe their emotions, but you feel them. You need to have strong boundaries, otherwise you will be overwhelmed by others' feelings. You also have the ability to shape-shift to appease whatever situation you are in, before you are even aware of it.

Being an empath can cause paralysis because there are so many outside influences, emotions, and opinions of others to process and grapple with. A key to my self-discovery and growth was when I read a book about a study of personality types called the Enneagram system. After taking the test many times, I recognized that I am personality type Five on the chart, and this was a monumental step forward in my own understanding of how I operate in the world. Also known as "observers" or investigators, Fives tend to wait until they have fully studied a subject or situation before feeling safe and comfortable enough to act. This has the potential for deep insights and powerful art but can be maddening to friends and especially impatient partners. The funny thing about dogs is they don't drain me like people can. Ever.

I never set out to be a storyteller, whether in photography, film, or writing. I have always been more of an observer. I notice details, patterns. I simply *feel* things. Being a shy kid, I really was left with no choice. I never fully understood why I could intuit things in such intricate ways—I simply knew that certain people would turn my stomach, and I knew I could never trust them.

I have always been an introvert that craves social experience. But extreme empathy or high sensitivity or however you want to describe it comes with a distinct need to recharge, as being in intense communion with other people will sap my energy dry. I don't need much, just a quiet space to refill my reservoir. Back in the dirtbag days, my van provided me with that, and now it could be a solo surf in the ocean, or simply the time I need daily to irrigate my colon. Two ex-girlfriends did not respect that time, and would come in and sit with me during my time that was reserved for only Earl and me. This was my personal time; it felt intrusive, as if I were cornered, as I could not go anywhere else.

After six months of intense self-work with Tatyana, instead of wanting to continue the relationship with Hannah, I recognized with little doubt that I needed out. My adrenals were taxed, I saw deep circles under my eyes, and my gray hairs were multiplying. For my own health and well-being, I needed to move on.

The day before Thanksgiving, Hannah and I had driven to the coast with my good friend Justin to surf and hang out. The three of us drove the ninety minutes to Manzanita in tense and awkward silence, and Justin and I dropped Hannah off at a coffee shop so she could work. Once we were alone, Justin looked at me and said, "I don't know what all is going on, but I don't want to see you suffer like this. It reminds me far too much of when I was trying to end my last relationship."

While Justin and I surfed that day, I tried to forget the situation, but knew I could not avoid the truth any longer. When Hannah rejoined us, the return ride was just as uncomfortable and tense. We dropped off Justin at his car and stopped at the market. Hannah looked at me and stated flatly, "I'll walk home."

As I pulled into my driveway I knew it was time.

The next evening, I went to the climbing gym and summoned the confidence finally to end it. As I arrived home, I took a deep breath at the door, bracing for the worst, and stepped inside.

I smelled freshly prepared food and glanced around the room. Candles were lit, and delicious aromas poured from the kitchen. *In Rainbows*, a favorite Radiohead album, was spinning on the turntable, a fire was crackling in the woodstove, and Hannah was sitting cross-legged on the couch and smiling at me with a calmness that was unsettling. I had entered the room feeling grounded, but then felt like I had entered an alternate reality—a life I had always dreamed of with her but that had never transpired.

Thrown off by the ambiance but determined to follow through with the breakup, I explained that I wanted to end things. She listened calmly, then spoke. "I saw another counselor today, and she told me that we're going to be together forever." I stared at her as if she were an alien being. "No," I said, "I need you to move your things out. Tomorrow."

Hannah finally did move out, and in the aftermath, I collapsed on my couch in cathartic relief, finally free of all the heaviness of the past year. Denali's cot creaked as he slowly stood up and hobbled over to me on unsteady legs. He rested his head in my lap and let out a long, theatrical sigh, looking up at me with eyes that said:

Finally! What in the world took you so long?

The stress and fighting are over, the air is clear,
and it's just you and me.

It was then I realized why Denali had been holding on for so long. He was looking out for me once again and had not wanted to leave me while I was in a relationship that he knew was no good for me. With that revelation, I held him for a long time, stroking his ears, and I thanked him for yet again being there during the times I most needed him.

In the damp and brief daylight hours of December, I curled up with Denali on his cot and looked into his eyes, clouded with age, yet still so kind. Those eyes were unflinching through every challenge, non-judgmental witnesses to the fourteen years and two months—over five thousand days—we had now shared.

He had been there through my despair over failing at marriage with Melanie, and all those moments when Denali stood guard while surgeries and chemotherapy drugs rendered me defenseless. He rolled his eyes and let out amused sighs while I pursued the intimacy of lovers who were in no way compatible with me. It was in those moments that Denali would switch to his aloof husky side and give my dates the cold shoulder. His stoic support was the only constant as I waded through the confusion of rebuilding a sense of self while living on the road in the van, and through the countless hours I stared through a loupe and light box over slide film, attempting to reinvent my career. Later on, the endless hours I stared blankly at my computer screen while editing and color correcting photographs must have seemed so silly to him.

I was there through it all, and I'd do it again! Okay, let's go for a walk. I want to go sniff that tree down the block and get the latest on the neighborhood happenings.

I petted his atrophied back, feeling his spine protruding as I ran my fingers through his fur along his hips and felt how much his once powerful thighs had deteriorated. Denali was physically fragile, yet still so noble in spirit. Aging could never take that away.

Denali had overcome abandonment at the shelter as a puppy and the insecurities that ensued, four cancerous mast cell tumors, a suffocating battle with laryngeal paralysis, and a confusing bout of idiopathic vestibular disease. Even though his body was now frail, his eyes still shone brightly with devotion and loyalty. Denali had done it all for me.

And I would gladly do it again!

I spoke gently with him, acknowledging all the years of joy and struggle he'd seen me through. My voice wavered and my eyes welled as I whispered in his soft ear, "It's okay to go now, friend. You've been with me through so much, through all of it, and for that I'm forever grateful. Please just tell me when it's time. I'm here for you. I love you. Thank you."

After my painful heart-to-heart with Denali, I decided to sit in an ayahuasca ceremony with Keith again, hoping to find some clarity from the recent months of turmoil. In the midst of the ceremony, a revelation hit me hard: In my adult life I had always had a companion, with Melanie and the serious relationships that followed the divorce.

Denali had been with me through it all, and now that it was his time to leave, I needed to stand tall and go on my own. He had walked me to the doorstep of the next era, a deeper version of manhood.

The evening that followed the ceremony was New Year's Eve, and I decided to take Denali to visit the coastline, where we had spent so much time together. I met up with my good friend Page Stephenson, whom I had recently hired to help with the video side of my business. In a continuation of the inner reflection I had started the night before, we ate magic mushroom chocolates and contemplatively strolled the beach after dark. It was a cold winter night, so I left Denali curled up next to the woodstove, where he could be warm and comfortable. The stars sparkled overhead, and with every step, sparks of bioluminescence in the sand exploded, lighting up the darkness. Chief Kiwanda Rock, a huge sea stack that sits just offshore, was shrouded in a thin fog. I stared at the rock, marveling at its fortitude, the way it had endured the intensity of winter storms over thousands of years. The mantra of the night before echoed in my mind: *Stand tall, be a man. Denali is leaving. For the first time in your adult life you'll be alone.*

You're strong enough on your own. Denali's own voice resonated within me. He always intuited when doubt paralyzed me.

I was acutely aware of how immensely Denali supported me over the years. I knew I could now do it on my own; I had no choice. Denali had helped me to grow and believe in myself enough that I had overcome my fears.

A nearby crabbing vessel lit up the rock, illuminating it in dramatic, cinematic fashion, a moment that would soon inspire us to use the rock as a backdrop for several scenes in my short film *Denali*.

The next morning, on New Year's Day 2014, we went surfing. The waves were as perfect as the crew that assembled in the lineup. My closest buddies and I surfed the point break waves inside the cape. Justin hollered in encouragement as I carved a high line on a golden, backlit wave. The wave faded out near the shore, and I kicked out over the top, realizing that everything would work out after all. Denali would always be a part of me.

The following week, I had a brainstorm session about an upcoming film project, one that had started out as more of a branded advertising piece about my love for climbing and the ocean but eventually shifted focus to the relationship between Denali and me. We sketched out a plan to capture footage with Denali in all of our favorite places. I hoped others would be able to relate to how much Denali had meant to me, and how he had helped me overcome challenges over the previous fourteen years. I knew the film would be a stress on Denali, but I also sensed the importance of capturing this footage of our last days together.

He and I had another heartfelt man-to-dog talk. I pressed my forehead to his and shared my thoughts with Denali. "I know your time is drawing near, and I am going to miss you so much. I love you, friend. I know I said it was okay for you to go, but I have one last favor to ask. Could you please stay strong for me, just through this month? By then we will have all the footage we need to tell our story. I know this will make you tired, but I'll do everything I can to help you! It would mean the world to me if you can hang on for this. I promise it will be the last thing I ever ask of you." I kissed his forehead and stared into his cloudy eyes. "Thank you, D! For everything."

I've got you, man. Whatever you need, I can do this!

During the filming Denali was often fatigued, yet even now when I watch the footage, I'm amazed at his strength in those final weeks. We filmed among the hallowed walls of Smith Rock, and on the open Oregon coast beaches with Chief Kiwanda Rock standing stoically in the background. These were two of the sacred places Denali and I had returned to time and time again, in spite of what these places had witnessed in my own struggles and failed relationships. The parallels between these two places were undeniable, and I knew it was imperative that they be represented in the Denali film.

As always, he was there for me, granting my final wish almost to the minute. Nearing midnight on a Friday evening, January 31, he began to develop the first symptoms of pneumonia. Over the next two days we would spend a weekend on that same beach in Pacific City where in years past we had played hours of fetch, watched sunsets, relished in joys, and grieved the heartaches. By Monday morning, he was gone.

As Denali slept fitfully during that last night, I sat on the edge of his cot and softly strummed a ukulele riff I had often practiced, and lyrics flowed where there had just been music:

As I sail away to the sea,
Please don't follow me.
As I sail away with the tide
I'll be by your side.
As I sail away to the sun
Please do not fear
for I'll be right here.

I had just started dating a woman named Whitney, a scientist who also climbed and surfed. She now was seeing me at one of the most vulnerable times in my entire life. I was crying softly, my face streaked with tears. Whit quietly sat on my couch and strummed my guitar as I lay next to Denali. My heart was heavy with the realization that it was time for him to go. I hated that I had to play a role in his departure, but I could not let him suffer.

My hands shook as I googled *home euthanasia*. I was in shock, my voice sounding far away when I spoke with the home care vet. "Yes, please come tomorrow morning." I began to sob. "It's time."

During Denali's final night, I did not sleep. Instead, I felt every raspy, labored breath as Denali lay on my chest. I comforted him and stroked his head throughout that long night. He was ready to go. Now it was my turn to return the favor and support him through his most vulnerable hours, as he had done countless times for me.

> Thank you, friend, I love you. Yes, I'm tired and am going away soon . . . but I'll never leave you. I'll always be here. You're strong now. You have all the strength within you to go on.

14

Accepting Grief

Denali had a presence about him. It was tangible in ways that are difficult to describe.

He had a quiet nobility, like that best friend who slips easily into your life before you realize "who" they are. Denali was warm and loving yet aloof and strong, an observer of every emotion and event yet free of attachment, selfless and always ready to move on to the next adventure. Stated simply, he was the best friend a man could ask for. To this day, the most difficult goodbye I ever have spoken was to Denali on his final morning. The memory is still heartrending, yet it affirms how our canine companions both simplify and expand our perceptions of how to give and accept the purest form of love.

No other being, not even family, knows us better or has seen us at our worst yet still loves and accepts us to their last breath. That's why losing them hurts so much and why it's a beautiful gift. What can I say about dogs? Their gaze is impervious to race, gender, political leaning, or beliefs. They see only the heart of the human behind the scars and history that formed their moral views and opinions.

A traumatic incident with or lack of exposure to the canine kind aside, I question the integrity of anyone who dislikes dogs. Denali was always correct in his judgment of character, seeing through the most seductive charm when I was blinded by it. I learned to watch his first impressions of those I met, and his approval would reinforce my own intuition. In this way he introduced me to lifelong friendships.

Denali's last night was a sleepless one for me. I relished in every second and cried softly as I stroked his head and shared my gratitude for his friendship. "You've been there for me through it all, old friend. You've taught me so much, and I know it's your time to go. Rest easy, friend. It will be hard but now I know I can stand on my own."

Thank you, friend. I'm so tired. And scared. Please stay with me until the end.

When the winter dawn finally lit the room, I gently carried Denali to his soft bed and continued comforting him until the veterinarian arrived. My sister came over to say goodbye and offer us support. I lay next to him and held him, and he licked my face one last time as the veterinarian prepared the injection to relax him. "Happy trails, my friend, thank you. I'll always love you." Denali took one last sigh and lay still, eliciting a geyser of tears from the depths of my being.

"He's gone." I hugged his limp body one last time, my own body trembling as I tried to hold back the sobbing. The vet and I carried Denali's lifeless frame down the steps to the back of her small SUV. I chuckled as I thought about all the dirtbag days Denali and I had shared. *Going out in style, I see. Thank you, my friend, for everything.*

I looked back as I walked up the steps to the house, feeling an emptiness I had never experienced. My sister gave me a hug, and I thanked her for being there for me. As the vet closed the back hatch of the SUV, a large crow flew low over my head, swooping down in a graceful arc not ten feet from the roof of the car. Every hair on my body stood up, recognizing the significance of that salute. Denali was saying goodbye. What I did not realize yet was that his life was just beginning to take flight.

A few hours passed, and I felt the urge to write about him. Words flowed effortlessly, and I wiped away the tears long enough to share this eulogy on Instagram in order to let Denali's many human friends know that he had passed:

Denali 1999–2014

This morning I said goodbye to my best friend after 14½ years of sharing adventure at my side. However difficult the transition, it's cause for reflection and a celebration of how much love and joy this incredible dog brought into my life.

Thank you, Denali, for giving me the courage to hit the road with a camera, a van, and no plan back in 2001, for never taking your eye off me through a year of cancer treatments, surgeries, and countless other challenges.

Thank you for your uncanny ability to walk into a frame at precisely the right moment to elevate an image, for teaching me patience and the joy in the simple quiet moments as I watched you grow older, and most of all, giving selflessly the unconditional love that only a true friend can give.

It's impossible to put into words all that you were and will always be to me—I was always convinced you were more human than dog, and all of the countless lives you touched felt the same.

Thank you for your unwavering belief in me, happy trails, my friend!

The hollowness I felt after losing Denali shocked me in its depth. There was a quiet loneliness upon awakening that lasted through the day, as I anticipated the familiar creaking of his cot and the clack of his nails as he skipped over to say hello. My anticipation of his greeting upon returning home was met with a hollow silence. While driving in my Element, I repeatedly glanced behind me to apologize to Denali for a sudden stop or the jarring noise as I drifted over a rumble strip. He hated the harsh vibrations of those more than anything.

I had lost my best friend, so the hurt seemed obvious, but the magnitude of the pain nearly paralyzed me. The grief was overwhelming and all-encompassing. Work became trivial, focus elusive.

The afternoon after Denali had passed, Isaac Brock called me, having heard about my loss. First, he made some obscure joke reference that only a mind as creative as his could connect, and then he was more direct. "How are you doing, man?"

"I'm doing okay, thanks for calling. I appreciate it," I answered.

"No, you're not okay. Come down to the studio, let's hang."

I spent the afternoon at the Modest Mouse studio, and Isaac's small yet deeply empathetic gesture got me out of the house and my head. It helped me process one of the toughest days of my life.

Tears kept blindsiding me, even long after my friends had acknowledged the loss and moved on.

When you lose a human friend or family member, other friends tend to understand that the road back is going to be long and challenging for you. But when a pet passes on, most can't comprehend or empathize with the time it takes to adjust to this new normal, the reality of the emptiness. They tend to quickly forget, and an undertone of "that happened, now get over it" quickly sets in. It's oddly similar to what happens following one's remission from cancer—that loneliness once you realize that life will never be the same.

A month after I lost Denali, it was still difficult for me to comprehend how the feelings of grief could be so sustained and intense. During a treatment with my acupuncturist, I mentioned to him how the tears just kept coming. He mused, "That's because your bond was so pure, he was there for you without question, and you for him. *That's true love*. With human relationships, there's baggage and resentment that both sides must overcome, but a dog harbors none of this. We love them, they love us. No strings attached, no baggage, just pure support no matter what. That's the definition of true love."

When you lose your canine soul mate, you not only lose the dog that has been your companion and friend through so much, but also have to let go of that chapter of your life, and who you were then. It forces you to grow into what you'll become, the last parting act of friendship.

———

ON A PHOTO SHOOT FOR A CLIMBING GEAR MANUFACTURER SET AMID THE stoic granite domes of Joshua Tree National Park, I wrapped up a shot, stepping away from the crew for a few moments alone. I hiked deep into a gully between two giant domes, finding privacy to take a leak and change out my colostomy bag. I took a few deep breaths and relished in a few moments of stillness, soaking in subtle sounds of the desert. I inhaled deeply and saw a movement in my peripheral vision. A large raven sat staring at me from a log not even five feet away. As I held my breath, the noble bird hopped closer, watching me intently. It cocked its head as we locked eyes. I exhaled slowly, and chills washed up my spine as I felt comforted by a familiar presence.

Denali was checking in, affirming he would never leave my side.

15

New Beginnings with Nori

The gut-wrenching grief of losing Denali was ever present but soft-ened by a new relationship I had begun with Whitney and her seven-year-old shepherd-hound rescue named Sadie. Whitney and I had started dating shortly after she had moved to Oregon from Colo-rado, after we had a conversation about climbing and surfing in Ore-gon. A couple of months after her move to Oregon, she wandered up on the beach while we were making the Denali film, and Sadie intro-duced herself by digging a sandy hole.

My first real date with Whit had been during Denali's last week-end, and Whit, Denali, Sadie, and I camped and surfed near Cape Kiwanda. Before his final breaths, Denali made sure I was not only free of a toxic relationship but beginning one that was healthier for me. It seemed a fitting final gesture for a friend who always looked out for me, even when I was oblivious to how he was trying to help.

The first day of that trip, Denali was his old self, walking slowly around the beach, meeting people, and begging for snacks as we surfed. When we woke up in camp on the second day, he refused food for the first time ever in his life, even ignoring canned tuna and some rotisserie chicken I bought for him. I knew then it was his time, and when we got back to the house that night, Denali gave me a look that made me know beyond a doubt that he was ready to go.

Two years later, Whitney and I had made the move to the Oregon coast, fulfilling my dream of living within walking distance of a surf break. With Chief Kiwanda Rock as the backdrop, Pacific City offered a gorgeous setting for both wave riding and sunset beach walks. As we packed, I assured Sadie that she would be in beach dog heaven and that she could "fish" to her heart's delight.

After the U-Haul was unloaded, I took a quick walk to the ocean with Sadie and noticed she was acting a bit lethargic and peeing far more often than normal. That night, as we slept in the new house on the river, Sadie drank bowl after bowl of water. Concerned, Whit took her in for an exam, and after glancing at the X-rays, the veterinarian recommended we take Sadie into the urgent care center in Portland for an ultrasound.

Whit drove in silence, and my heart felt heavy with premonition as Sadie lay on the bed platform in the back of the Honda Element. She lay in a regal posture, as if to embody one final show of strength and support to her human companions. Sadie licked my arm for quite some time, then let out a sigh of acceptance before standing up and turning around and round. As she settled down once more, I could sense that she was in pain, and I tried to comfort her. I could feel that her stomach was bloated, but for Whit's sake I stayed as optimistic as I could.

Minutes crawled as we waited for the vet to return to the examination room. When she did, her visage was somber, matching her black shirt and darkly painted fingernails. She motioned for Whit and me to follow her to the ultrasound room, and as we entered, Sadie lay on her side, belly shaved on the cold exam table.

Both the vet and her tech looked grim, glancing up sadly at us as they explained the images on the screen. "This is her liver and spleen, and all these large spots in both are cancer. I'm so sorry to tell you this, but if you try to take her home, she may bleed out and it would be a horribly painful way for her to go."

I was shocked as, just hours earlier, Sadie had been exploring the tide pools and running along the same beach where Denali had spent his final days, and now it seemed that she would never return. I did my best to comfort Whit and help her in making the difficult choice with this sudden cruel news.

Once more I found myself in tears holding Whit and hugging her sweet canine companion as Sadie took her last breath on a blanket between us on the tile floor. Heartbroken from the loss of a second dog in such a short time, I knew I would need more time before considering adopting another.

Whit was working in Colorado for the summer, and the house seemed so vacant without a dog's energy. During those aches of loneliness, I began to realize just how integral a dog's friendship was to my needs. I had started perusing adoption listings on Petfinder and wondered if I could ever find another dog that I could connect with on a soul level like Denali. I took a trip to the main animal shelter in Portland, but the visit only left me more confused. It felt more like a competition than a search for a true companion, as I was only given a few minutes with the dogs I thought could be a good fit before the next potential adoptees were given their time. Most of the more desirable mixes and breeds had a waiting list three or four people deep. I decided to have an open heart and knew the right pup would find me without needing to force things.

On the Monday after the Fourth of July weekend, Whitney was coming home to visit. Before boarding her early morning flight in Denver, Whit sent a simple one-line text message:

Check out this cute puppy ☺

My expectations low, I sighed as I clicked the Petfinder link. As the first image downloaded, I thought my heart was going to explode from my chest. Nori's markings bore an uncanny resemblance to Denali's, but her eyes were what struck me most. Within her soft gaze I sensed an old soul, and even though I was not yet ready for a dog, somehow I just knew she was the one who could fill the void I had felt since losing Denali.

I knew I had to act without hesitation, and while sitting on the toilet completing my daily colon flush I crafted a lengthy email to My Way Home Dog Rescue, which was fostering the puppy. I described my relationship with Denali and how I would give Nori a similar life of adventure. I mentioned that I lived two hours away but would be coming out to visit Nori as soon as I picked up my girlfriend from the airport.

Twenty-five minutes into my two-hour drive to the airport, I was passing the first dairy farms near Tillamook, and my iPhone ringtone interrupted my train of thought. I picked it up to hear the voice of Cheryl, the puppy's foster mom, on the line. She was excited to tell me that she had seen my film about Denali when it was released, and that the film had helped her through her own struggle with and recovery from cancer.

I picked up Whit from her flight and told her we needed to head straight to My Way Home. After Cheryl greeted us, she hollered toward the house to alert Nori that she could come out. A bundle of fur burst out of the sliding door and beelined her way over to Whit and me, rolling around excitedly at my feet.

Cheryl explained that Nori had been found with her mother and litter, all feral, in the desert of California's Central Valley at two months of age. She was extremely shy and skittish around people, hiding behind the furniture for much of her time in foster.

Nori seemed friendly in spite of her past and, curious about her personality, I ran into the grassy yard as she tore after me, chasing me in circles around a bush. I lay down suddenly, and Nori paused to drape her soft puppy body over my head, content just to lie there. It was a quiet moment of connection and enough to confirm that this was indeed the pup I had been dreaming of.

On her very first day at home, I brought Nori to the beach, the same place that Denali had spent his last days. Life comes full circle more often as time goes on.

In the ensuing weeks, each hour melted any hesitations I had about welcoming another dog into my heart. I had resigned myself to feeling that no other dog would ever live up to Denali, but this little one was reminding me of the joy that dogs can bring us with her every silly antic.

Only three months old, Nori needed constant attention and was a reminder of the crazy, sleepless realities of adopting a puppy, yet having her in my life was worth any inconvenience. I was emphatically in love with living near the ocean, and each new excursion and beach adventure was made richer with Nori frolicking at my side. I was in the early phases of convincing myself that writing this book was worthwhile, and her excited nudges to get outside for a beach romp helped keep me out of my self-doubt and swirling thoughts as I stared at the keyboard each afternoon.

As the days with her stretched to months, I began to see many of the same traits I had loved so dearly in Denali. The similarities began in her soulful eyes and coloring, and her widow's peak crown and eye-liner markings, but mostly I saw them in her little personality quirks. Denali was independent yet always wanted to be nearby and was super affectionate. Nori is similar—she's very attentive but is confident and balanced, and she possesses a gentle sweetness that some say comes only with a female pup.

A quiet bond with each of our canine companions forms over time, but my connection with Nori seemed to happen more rapidly. Maybe it was the stability and caring less about what others think of us that comes in our fourth decade of life, but Nori and I seemed to find our rhythm immediately.

I shared the news of my new companion on social media and mused publicly that maybe I should change her name for her new life with me. Belinda Baggs, a well-traveled Australian longboard surfer whom Denali and I had adventured with often, said that *naminori* meant "wave ride" or "surfing" in Japanese, and that I had to keep the name. As I dug further into the name Nori, I found there was a depth far beyond edible seaweed, however appropriate with our life by the sea, that suited her.

During Gerry Lopez's snow surfing event on Mount Bachelor, I was snowboarding with several of the riders from Gentemstick, a snow surf manufacturer based in the Japanese snow-riding mecca of Hok-kaido, and they were so animated upon learning Nori's name. "*Yukinori!*"

one exclaimed. "Snow rider!" Another said, "*Yokonori!* Board rider—snowboard surfboard skateboard."

I used to call Denali "Nali," so Nori feels similar and familiar in that way, too, and even though today I still slip and call her Denali, she does not hold it against me.

Nori has made me aware of all the things that I had not even realized were missing and how much I needed new canine companionship for my own healing and closure. Life simply feels complete now. My walls have crumbled completely, and I must admit that I had forgotten how to love after Denali had gone, and that Nori showed up to lead the way.

Denali had seen me through the age of dial-up internet, landlines, mobile flip phones, and slide film scanners. He became accustomed to my long photo-editing sessions when digital photography turned me into my own photo-processing lab. But he was not all that pleased when the first smartphones were introduced, after I began staring at a tiny glowing screen for hours every day. The early Blackberry devices were a life changer for a freelancer like me, enabling me to answer emails from the climbing crag, ski lift, or trailhead, and freeing me from the confines of a laptop, office hours, and finding coffee shops or libraries on the road.

Wi-Fi was not a thing yet during my early van years, but it became more prevalent later on. Most networks were wide open back then, no passwords required, so I would drive my van through neighborhoods and camp out front of whichever establishment had the strongest signal. During his later years, Denali would often give me that knowing look of resignation and disgust when I stared at my phone for hours, and wonder what had happened to his old adventure buddy that used to spend the majority of his time outdoors.

By the time I adopted Nori, iPhones had fully taken over as powerful computing devices full of algorithmically appealing apps that we keep in our pockets. For many of us, they have become a new addiction to grapple with, and before Night Shift mode reduced the blue light exposure in the evenings, they interrupted our nights and sleep as well as our waking hours. Nori is less patient with my iPhone time and has no qualms about letting me know. She will crawl over to me in bed, slap the offending device from my hand, and lay her head on my chest to bring my attention to scratching her ears. Once she has had her fill, she will insistently jump off the bed and do laps to the door until we go to the beach.

Many have claimed that each person has only one heart dog or canine soul mate. Nori has proved to me that this concept needs to be expanded to allow new love in. I know this to be true with human relationships too. Some who come into our lives simply open up our hearts to love, while others nurture us through dark times or push us to grow, and our pups often introduce us to other humans that become lifelong friends.

Whether for one hour or for over a decade, those canines or humans who we allow deep into our hearts are exactly what we need at that time. Denali was a challenging, independent, and nurturing being that stood by me through a ridiculous amount of growing up. Nori shares the old soul and thirst for adventure that Denali possessed, yet is gentler and more tolerant of my quirks. She is precisely what I need in my life right now, and is also a reflection of my own evolution as an individual. Our dogs are mirrors, for better or worse.

I am now fifteen years out from my diagnosis, and my oncologists say that my cancer is 100 percent gone at this point and there is very little chance of a recurrence of the same tumor. I feel the fact that I survived and am still alive is a blessing that I should think on every day for perspective, and it serves as a reminder to make the most of every moment. It hits me hardest whenever I hear of someone losing their battle with this horrible disease, especially those who also had colorectal cancer. It always reminds me not to take my time here for granted. It's a feeling that many survivors can relate to, that whenever I have any health issue, it's easy to overreact. Recently I had a suspicious mole on my back examined by a dermatologist, and it was challenging not to immediately default to the worst-case scenario, a malignant melanoma. The mole ended up being okay, but every checkup and visit to the doctor continues to be a nerve-racking experience of wondering, *What if this is cancer again?*

I feel that attitude is everything. A cancer diagnosis is a life-or-death battle with so many variables completely out of our control, and our attitude toward it is a choice. We can either let the negative aspects of the situation overwhelm us, or we can focus on doing what we can to keep on the path of survival. A smile can rise above the horrific nausea and pain.

On that same note, it's important to surround yourself with those who can treat you normally and get you outside or spend time with you when you are feeling down and unmotivated. When I was super nauseated from chemo, if I was up for it, I would sometimes just go to Smith Rock and not even climb, as just being around friends in the sunshine and fresh air was a huge lift to my spirits.

I firmly believe that my cancerous tumor was triggered by stress, the internalization of the feelings of pain, betrayal, and failure, triggering mutations at the cellular level. I now prioritize eliminating negative relationships from my life. It is not only to enjoy a more pleasant life, it is for my health, for my very existence and survival.

Self-care is so important, and it is essential to lead a life that will lift you up. Cling to the positive and let go of the negative. Your life depends on it. As conservationist and grizzly bear activist Doug Peacock said to me recently, "Arm yourself with friendship."

For nearly five years Whit and I had shared passions for sheer rock walls, peeling waves, and filmmaking. I had hoped we could work through our differences and challenges, but ultimately my intuition made me listen to my heart and I made the difficult decision to break things off. It had been the longest relationship of my life, but I held no resentment or regret, only a burning feeling that it was time to move forward.

Through the pain I felt in the breakup with Whit, I am reminded that there is no failure other than the failure to try, or the failure to open up your heart to hurt, to love, to seize opportunities, or to take risks. I also know the greatest growth has come through the most painful experiences.

I first went to Smith Rock with Melanie and continued visiting in the two decades since, loving my time there even after that heartbreak. The two relationships that followed ended just as unceremoniously, yet I still love Smith Rock and refuse to let those experiences alter how special the place is to me. I feel the same about the beaches and surf breaks I now frequent. Heartbreak, new beginnings, and continual transition, these shores have observed them all, only to be renewed by an incoming tide.

Rewrite your story, over and over. That is the essence of growth, of life.

Those who never have to face the fire never truly experience the full breadth of emotion. From my soul-crushing heartbreaks to the struggles to begin and sustain a creative career and my battle through cancer, each challenge taught me deep lessons and encouraged a growth that an "easy" life could never do.

With a friend by my side like Denali, I could endure more and simply enjoy every moment more fully, and Nori has already done the same for me. And the dog hugs . . . I would often press my forehead to Denali's in an exchange of love, and Nori is ever receptive to this as well. She is even more enthusiastic about hugs than Denali was, and as soon as she is invited, she will throw her arms around my neck and just lean in. It nearly makes me cry with joy every time. There are even times it seems when the quiet moments of connection with our dogs can feel even more precious than those any human can offer.

So, hold your friends close, listen to your heart, and let yourself be vulnerable, because it is there that the best and the truest experiences will manifest.

The adjustment to singlehood has now set in once more, and for two years I have been living full time in the camper van I built out with my father a few years ago. The van has become my quiet space to write this book, while at the same time enabling me to save toward the home that I am currently building at the beach to share with friends and pay forward all the generosity of those who have hosted me.

As I prepared to settle in for the evening, I swept off the beach sand that had accumulated from the day and slipped under the covers on my comfy latex mattress for the night. Nori hopped up lightly to join me, nestling her slender frame against my side and the vacant pillow to my left, then rested her chin on my chest and sighed through closed eyes.

Under the weight of her head, I inhaled a deep breath of my own and stared into the dim light at the tongue-and-groove cedar ceiling of my tiny home on wheels. *Yeah, I might be a forty-something-year-old single guy living in his van with his dog,* I mused, recognizing the many ways I was right back where my journey began with Denali, *but you know, I'm so good with that!*

I looked at Nori, her eyes still closed in a contented state. "What do you think?" I asked her. She opened one eye, stared for a moment, drew a long inhale, and let out another contented sigh.

"Thank you, Nori," I whispered as I gave her another sleepy hug.

It's just you and me, Nori. Just you and me.

Denali Lives On

As I climbed upward through the steep moves of Chain Reaction at Smith Rock, utilizing movements rehearsed over hundreds of ascents, memories of my recently departed companion emanated from the pocket of my blue jeans, where I had stashed a small bag of Denali's ashes. I reached the final moves of the pitch and clipped into the anchors, and as I sat back against the tension of my rope, a warm ray of evening sunlight wove its way between the two volcanic parapets that made up the castle-like rock formation to the west. I pulled out the ashes and was mesmerized as the powder slipped through my chalky fingers. Flecks of carbonized flesh and bone sparkled in iridescent patterns as they fell slowly to the earth, rising and falling with the breaths of wind over the high-desert landscape. I glanced down and noticed a climber watching me. He looked vaguely familiar, someone I recognized from the climbing gym and music shows around Portland.

A week later, I visited Smugglers Cove, a half-mile-long stretch of southwest-facing beach that is known to surfers as Short Sands. Popular with the Portland surf- and beach-loving crowds, the lineup would often be congested on sunny weekend days when the surf fore-cast appeared favorable. I paddled my surfboard quietly outside of the crowded peak I had been surfing and pulled a small waterproof pouch from the inside of the neoprene sleeve of my wetsuit. As I poured the contents into the clear waters of the Pacific Ocean, Denali's ashes swirled and glittered in the current as they sank from view. I turned to my right only to see the same face that I had seen while releasing Denali's ashes at Smith Rock staring inquisitively in my direction.

The chances of the same individual witnessing these deeply personal moments in two locations nearly five hours apart from one another was too serendipitous to ignore. I introduced myself to Matt, and we soon became frequent climbing and surf buddies. Matt's friendship and ar-chitectural skills have proved instrumental. He and I collaborated on the design for my new home that I am building, just steps from the very same beach where Denali spent his final days. Even though Denali's physical form has departed, he is still helping me make new friends.

Shortly after I released Denali's ashes, I was invited to Austin dur-ing SXSW for a book release with Jeff Johnson and James Joiner when I received a text from the incredibly gifted filmmaker and my good friend Ben Knight. I had asked him to help craft the edit of the short film on my relationship with Denali, but he had been struggling with the concept and had gone completely silent.

Making the film had already been a deeply introspective yearlong saga for me before I hired Ben. I had thrown out several edits and was deep in debt but unable to move on with my life until I finished the film. The significance of the bond Denali and I shared through so many trying and formative experiences was evident in the tears that had flowed freely during that year. In experiencing that grief, I felt deeply that I needed to share Denali's story in hopes that it could touch others who have experienced a similar feeling of support in a friendship through hard times. I could not let go until the film felt like an extension of the love I felt for Denali.

I joked that it was a stretch to trust a cat lover like Ben to tell the story of me and my dog, but I knew deep down in my gut that he was the perfect fit to craft the story. He had a skater rebel side to him but a softhearted and witty way of making films. I was confident that he would nail the tone and prevent it from feeling too cheesy. I had not heard from him in weeks and I was growing increasingly concerned that he was going to bail from the project.

Ben's text read: Check your email. Please find a quiet spot to watch and use headphones.

Like many wonderfully creative people, Ben prefers to work in isolation. I typically sit in on edits for my film collaborations, but for this one I was in the dark. I had no idea what to expect when I clicked on the private Vimeo link he had just sent over. I had given him full liberty to go as deep and personal with my story as was necessary. I trusted his instincts to tell it in the most graceful way possible, yet I still fully expected to be disappointed. How could anyone capture in a short film the love and friendship I had shared with my best friend for fourteen and a half years?

I was in the back seat of a rental car and popped in headphones to watch. A minute into the film, the screen of my iPhone was nearly obscured by big sloppy tears. By the end of the film I was almost sobbing, yet I felt an immense relief. Jeff and James looked over at the awkward mess I had become, and asked, "How is it?"

"Amazing. This cut is incredible," I said. Ten minutes later, I showed it to them in the hotel and I held my breath for most of the film. As the credits rolled, I glanced over at them and to my surprise,

I saw two men crying openly, tears soaking their faces. *Hmmm,* I thought. *This is hitting closer to home than I expected.*

Later that afternoon, I was sitting at a table outside a busy café with Alexandria Bombach, another filmmaker who was in Austin premiering her feature *Frame by Frame*, a documentary on photography in Afghanistan during the Taliban regime. She had known Denali quite well in his later years, so I handed her my phone and headphones and asked for her honest opinion on Ben's edit. I sat there feeling vulnerable as she watched. A few minutes into watching, Alexandria started to sob so loudly that people walking by the café stopped to see what was wrong.

It felt incredible to have Denali's story come to life so vividly in the film. Cathartic tears were released with each new screening, and I cried uncontrollably the first twenty or thirty times I saw the film. It was a vulnerable experience sharing intimate details about my life, in particular the part about my colostomy bag. I had never shared this part of myself publicly before, and I had no idea how that would be received by those outside my friend circle.

The first public screening of the film was at 5Point Film Festival, an intimate single-screen festival held each year in the outdoor recreation mecca of Carbondale, Colorado. With all eight hundred attendees watching the same films together in one room, the festival has a more intimate community feeling than many of the larger festivals.

A few years after my first forays into shooting motion, I had been invited to be the featured photographer for 5Point Film Festival, and I felt like a fish out of water. I was within my outdoor industry community, yet I felt I did not belong at all with the filmmakers who were present. I saw short films that moved me with their simple artistry, but never dreamed I could do the same. That all changed when I sat down to eat lunch and a guy named Skip Armstrong sat next to me. He had just premiered two of his own short adventure films from the Of Souls + Water series, and I was impressed with how they felt deeper than most of the highlight reel films I had seen in the surf and climbing worlds. Skip was friendly, striking up a conversation that led to my first director role, for an experimental music video for the song "Minor Cause" by Emancipator. We used a drone for the piece, an eight-bladed octocopter that could fly for only ninety seconds before it had to be landed to change all eight batteries.

Two years later, Skip would help film my short film *Denali*, a collaboration that would forever change my life. We have become close friends and frequent collaborators in the years that followed. During the film premiere, I sat between Ben Knight and Skip, and they both had their arms around me in support as I tried to quell my feelings of nakedness and vulnerability.

It was terrifying to share my story publicly, but I knew there was a universal theme in the film that was much greater than my friendship with Denali. The efforts to make the film began as an act of my own closure, but I hoped others could relate. As the film began to play, I thought, *If just one person will be helped by me sharing this story, it will be all be worth it.*

As the credits for *Denali* rolled, Ben, Skip, and I crouched in the theater wings for the Q&A after the film. I hurriedly wiped away tears, trying to compose myself before taking the stage. In the dim reflection of the credits, I saw that hundreds of red-eyed audience members were doing the same.

After the screening, a woman in a wheelchair who I found out later was an ex–pro skier approached me and offered me the warmest hug. "Thank you, thank you, thank you, I needed that so much. I had two huskies, and losing them, my best friends, was even harder for me than being paralyzed."

Then and there, I felt satisfied that the year and a half of struggle to find the proper depth and tone for the film had all been worth it. A day later, when the winners of the festival were announced, *Denali* ended up sweeping the 5Point accolades, and we were presented with both the People's Choice and the Best of Festival jury awards. To me, the film was so personal that I previously had not been able to see beyond my story, but after that festival screening, I realized we had made a film that was unique from a cinematic perspective as well.

———

SURVIVAL IS A FUNNY THING. WHEN ROGUE CELLS WREAKED HAVOC ON THE end of my digestive tract, my future was unceremoniously stripped away, and I had no choice but to focus on the realities of staying alive. Staring down my mortality, I found within myself an untapped reservoir of fortitude that somehow stood above the ever-present fear and crippling nausea. Each day, I had to rise in spite of the heavy metals and radioactive particles that were lobbed at my tumor like Molotov cocktails. Family and friends made valiant efforts to help, but no matter what they said or did, it was still my battle alone to fight.

During those trying months, Denali never let me out of his sight. When I had no energy for even the most basic communication, he would curl up next to me and offer his wordless support. With the nurses' blessing, he would crawl ever so gently into my hospital bed, carefully lying down so as to not disturb my healing incisions or the IV lines that dangled from the headboard. In my lowest moments, his actions resonated deep in my being, and his support helped me to keep on fighting when the vomiting left me weak and too demoralized to ask for help. Several years and countless adventures later, when Denali developed cancer, I had the chance to return the favor. His companionship was a steady, grounding place where I could find my footing during a turbulent time.

I hoped the film would honor his friendship and the profound effect he had on me, and that it would capture the essence of our bond and our respective battles with cancer. Narrated from his perspective, it seemed to touch anyone who had ever loved a pet or lost a loved one.

Six weeks after premiering the film at festivals, we released the film online. The response that followed the film's release was utterly overwhelming and unexpected. The first day, my friends were sharing it on social media, and the film received about five thousand views, a modest number, but I was just grateful to finally have it out in the world. That night, I slept in my backyard. When the heat of the summer sun woke me, I turned on my phone and I thought it might explode with all the incoming messages. I had voicemails from publications across the US and London, the *Today* show, BuzzFeed, and local news anchors. I checked the view count that night, and it had already hit one million. In its first week online, it was viewed more than eight million times, and I had lost my voice from the endless interviews.

I received thousands of heartfelt emails and Facebook messages, and Oprah featured the film on her television show *SuperSoul Sunday*. *Denali* has since been screened at film festivals worldwide, winning several honors, and it has continued to touch hearts. As of this writing, it has been seen more than eighteen million times online, and there has been considerable interest in making a feature film, with inquiries coming from several major studios in Hollywood as well as established directors and producers.

The response was so far beyond any expectation I ever could have had. It was a true testament to the depth of friendship Denali and I shared. He was with me through so much and never once wavered.

The film was only the briefest snapshot of our story, but it captured the feeling in a way I appreciated. I thought back to the many weeks I had spent digging through old images and scanning negatives and slide film, searching for moments that could help convey our friendship. When my mom dug out a few long-lost photographs she had shot of Denali in my hospital bed, I knew they were the key I was seeking to unlock the story.

I recently came across a text message exchange with Ben Knight, regarding the challenges of bringing the Denali film to life:

Ben:

I'm sorry for being defensive at times, I just feel the need to at least explain my thought process on some things

Me:

It is all I really wanted for this piece . . . for someone to recognize the depth of my relationship with Denali and truly see the full potential for and universal themes of the story. It means the world to me to collaborate with you on this, a friend that I have the utmost respect and trust in.

Ben:

I still feel lucky that you didn't leave a burning bag
of poop on my doorstep

Me:

I had this nagging feeling that you were the "one"
for this film a year ago, and I'm so glad that it all
worked out.

Your rare and insanely wonderful combination of
intuition, sensitivity, talent, and skillful storytelling,
blended with who you are as a person, made this a
piece that is not only incredible and moving, but
one that will resonate deeply to countless others
and has the ability to transcend the subject matter
and touch anyone who's endured hardship, had a
loss or felt the power and love of friendship.

You made a work of art, my friend.

It's so personal, yet you made something that is so
much bigger than Denali and I. This makes it really
easy to take myself and my insecurities out of the
picture, and to share it with anyone and everyone.
Thank you.

I am so grateful for both Ben and Skip for their friendship and
support, for seeing the potential in the story, and for putting the care
and heart into using their talents to make this piece come to life. This
film was a collaboration, and I feel like our friendships shine through

in the final piece. It was an extremely difficult story for me to share, but working with friends who cared about me made it easier to trust and allowed me to be vulnerable about my story.

I had hoped the story would resonate, and the response was nothing short of overwhelming.

A year later, after I received all of the emails and messages from people who saw the film after it became public, I realized this film was more than the story of a man and his dog. We had explored the universal themes of friendship and loss, and created a narrative about overcoming the challenges we all face in life, including facing a disease as indiscriminate as cancer. The unquestioning friendship of a dog is relatable to nearly everyone, and Denali unlocked a lot of hearts and tears. Having such a positive reception made the struggles in finishing the film feel truly worthwhile, and now Denali lives on in the hearts of so many.

I am a private person, so sharing such a personal story with millions of people has been both incredibly affirming and challenging. The impact of so many people suddenly feeling they knew me and could relate to my story was exhausting, and it was impossible to respond to all of the messages. The film, which showed just a small glimpse of what Denali and I experienced together, resonated so deeply with so many and taught me so much about the power of vulnerability that I decided to explore our friendship and the hardships we overcame together in this memoir.

———

TODAY'S STANDARD MEDICAL PROTOCOL OF RECOMMENDING THAT PATIENTS wait until fifty years of age to go for their first colonoscopy still infuriates me. I met Tate MacDowell, a fellow colorectal cancer patient in his early thirties, through a mutual friend at Patagonia after he needed advice about living with a colostomy. He nicknamed me his "stomentor" for helping him deal with his new stoma. His tumor, an advanced stage II, was exactly the same stage as mine, but higher up in his colon so he was later able to reverse the colostomy. Soon after he was given the all clear, his cancer came back and is now stage IV metastatic. Tate's motto "No wasted time" as he fights for his life, and his watercolor series of the same name, inspire me every day.

Last year I learned that two incredible young women that I had shared my story with and offered advice to during their individual battles with colon cancer both had succumbed to the disease. Amanda was thirty-four, and Heather had only just turned thirty.

Cancer is indiscriminate and cruel. I can clearly recall my conversations with each of them, assuring them that a cancer diagnosis and dealing with colostomy bags were obstacles they could overcome. So why did Heather and Amanda succumb to the same disease I encountered? Why, as a young father and husband, is Tate now fighting for his life against this disease for a second time? Why am I still here? This question baffles me even today and motivated me to share my experience in detail in this book. If I can help just one person overcome this disease, overcome an obstacle in life, or get in to see a doctor before it is too late, writing this book will have been worth every moment.

Each and every individual who receives a cancer diagnosis endures a unique personal struggle. Cancer touches nearly all of us in some way, and by sharing Denali's struggles and mine, my hope is that others can relate and draw strength from our journey. The treatments that shattered my dignity were unspeakably challenging yet taught me lessons that I carry to this day. Lessons that speak to life well beyond cancer. Healing is a process that can take decades, and only now, fifteen years later, do I feel qualified to articulate what I learned by running that gauntlet.

One facet of cancer that is often overlooked by doctors, patients, and caregivers is that surviving cancer is sometimes more challenging than the awful treatments themselves. The emotional roller coaster of detoxing from chemotherapy cocktails and radiation treatments, the fright of a wide-open future, and the shock of friends suddenly moving on after the wonderful news of your remission after months of those same friends pouring on their love and support are some of the hardest things I have endured.

Dose after dose of the toxic cocktail of lifesaving poison left me with sweat that reeked of heavy metals. My emotions were like a fifteen-year-old's, swinging dramatically from joy to despair. Survivorship can be a cruel awakening to the reality of an uncertain and sometimes daunting future. This is an ironic twist considering the Zen-like approach needed to survive the misery of cancer treatments. To survive, there is no option but to focus only on each moment. The future beyond the current round of chemo and the subsequent toxic treatments is too overwhelming to even consider.

A friend once confided that her mother survived breast cancer, only to tragically take her own life shortly after. This brought me to realize that I was far from alone in my own struggle to return to what is considered a "normal" life after cancer.

The fourteen and a half years of friendship I shared with Denali were rich in adventure and joy, growing together through the obstacles we all face in life. He stood by me through the anguish of divorce and a life-threatening illness, accompanying me through the many chapters of my life while navigating me to a more grounded adulthood.

During my formative years, between twenty-four and thirty-nine, he walked me through heartbreak into a career as a professional adventure photographer and filmmaker and to the very door of my forties, where on rickety, arthritic limbs he stood by and saw me out of a toxic relationship before finally letting go.

Denali was one of those special creatures who seemed to know me better than I know myself. He was a magical soul, and it's no exaggeration to say that he helped me to show up in the world, wearing my scars and weaknesses without shame so that I might help others through their own battles in this journey of life. Anyone who has been lucky enough to have that one special dog who stood by their side during a stretch of critical years knows what I'm talking about.

I think that Denali knew his purpose, approaching life with curiosity and always being open to its boundless possibility.